Applied Artificial Neural Network Methods for Engineers and Scientists

Solving Algebraic Equations

T0338637

Applied Artificial Neural Network Methods for Engineers and Scientists

Solving Algebraic Equations

Snehashish Chakraverty
Sumit Kumar Jeswal

National Institute of Technology Rourkela, India

 World Scientific

NEW JERSEY · LONDON · SINGAPORE · BEIJING · SHANGHAI · HONG KONG · TAIPEI · CHENNAI · TOKYO

Published by

World Scientific Publishing Co. Pte. Ltd.

5 Toh Tuck Link, Singapore 596224

USA office: 27 Warren Street, Suite 401-402, Hackensack, NJ 07601

UK office: 57 Shelton Street, Covent Garden, London WC2H 9HE

British Library Cataloguing-in-Publication Data
A catalogue record for this book is available from the British Library.

**APPLIED ARTIFICIAL NEURAL NETWORK METHODS FOR
ENGINEERS AND SCIENTISTS**
Solving Algebraic Equations

ISBN 978-981-123-020-2 (hardcover)
ISBN 978-981-123-021-9 (ebook for institutions)
ISBN 978-981-123-022-6 (ebook for individuals)

For any available supplementary material, please visit
https://www.worldscientific.com/worldscibooks/10.1142/12097#t=suppl

Desk Editor: Rhaimie Wahap

Typeset by Diacritech Technologies Pvt. Ltd.
Chennai - 600106, India

Printed in Singapore

Contents

Preface

Algebraic equations play important and challenging roles in diversified fields of science and engineering. These engineering and science problems usually reduce to different algebraic equations. It is worth mentioning that algebraic equations are of various types such as polynomial, transcendental and Diophantine equations, linear and nonlinear systems of equations, linear and nonlinear eigenvalue problems, etc. There exist different analytical and numerical methods to handle these algebraic equations. However, these equations may sometimes be difficult to solve using traditional analytical/numerical methods due to the presence of singularity or complexity of the functions. Moreover, sometimes these methods may be problem-dependent and may fail to give a converged solution with particular discretization.

In recent decades, soft computing techniques such as Artificial Neural Network (ANN)-based methods have been developed to handle algebraic equations. These ANN-based methods may be seen as an alternative approach and, in some cases, these methods may be advantageous over the existing analytical/numerical methods.

The main aim of this book has been to introduce expert ANN methods to handle different algebraic equations. As such, the book starts with the basics of ANN along with different mathematical preliminaries with respect to algebraic equations. Then it addresses ANN-based methods for solving different algebraic equations viz. polynomial equations, transcendental equations, Diophantine equations, linear and nonlinear systems of equations, eigenvalue problems, definite integrals, etc. to handle a variety of application problems. Different numerical examples and application problems have been solved using the ANN procedure. Convergence plots and/or convergence tables of the results have also been depicted to show the efficacy of these ANN methods. It is worth mentioning that various application problems viz. Bakery problem, Power electronics applications, Pole placement, Electrical network analysis, Structural engineering problems, etc. have also been investigated applying the said method(s). As such, this book consists of eleven chapters. Brief ideas related to each chapter are discussed as follows.

Chapter 1 includes preliminaries related to ANN. Different ANN architectures, learning rules and activation functions have been presented here. Mathematical preliminaries related to different algebraic equations have been discussed in Chapter 2. Polynomial, transcendental and Diophantine equations, linear and nonlinear systems of equations, linear and nonlinear eigenvalue problems have been defined in Chapter 2. In Chapter 3, a four-layer ANN architecture with a detailed procedure based on the concept of backpropagation algorithm has been presented for solving polynomial equations. Efficiency of the ANN procedure has been shown by solving few numerical examples and an application problem for a Bakery. ANN-based approach for solving transcendental equations has been addressed in Chapter 4. Simple numerical examples with an application problem of power electronics have been considered in this context. A multi-layer ANN model along with a step-by-step description for solving Diophantine equations has been incorporated in Chapter 5. Standard numerical examples with an application problem of pole placement have been included in this regard. Chapter 6 addresses a single-layer ANN model for solving linear systems of equations. Numerical examples and an application of static structural problems have been investigated to show the efficiency of the ANN method. Further, an ANN technique for handling nonlinear systems of equations has been presented in Chapter 7, where numerical examples and an application problem related to electrical network analysis have been examined. A multi-layer ANN architecture for solving linear eigenvalue problems has been constructed in Chapter 8. As such, numerical examples and application of structural dynamics have been investigated here. Chapter 9 includes an ANN method for solving nonlinear eigenvalue problems and incorporates a solution for a numerical example as well as an application problem of structural dynamics. Chebyshev Neural Network (ChNN) method for solving definite integrals has been addressed in Chapter 10, where related numerical examples and an application problem of fluid force on a vertical surface have been handled. Finally, Chapter 11 presents an ANN approach for solving inverse problems.

The present book addresses systematic understanding of ANN method(s) in order to solve various algebraic equations. Application problems from different subject areas are considered to demonstrate the applicability of the ANN methods by solving the governing algebraic equations. The authors do believe that the book will prove to be a benchmark for graduate and postgraduate students, teachers, engineers, researchers and industry in the mentioned subject areas with respect to the application of the recent ANN methods. The book provides comprehensive results, up to date and self-contained reviews of the topic along with application-oriented treatment of the use of newly developed ANN methods for different domains of engineering and sciences. It is certain that the readers will find this important book an outstanding source to solve a variety of problems concerning algebraic equations through alternative method(s) in one place, which may be helpful for further thought-provoking research in different directions.

Acknowledgments

This book may have not been possible without the continuous support, encouragement and motivation received from various wonderful people around us. To begin with, we would like to thank first, all the researchers and authors mentioned (included) in the references who have directly or indirectly helped us to do research in this subject area and then write the book in a concise and fruitful manner.

The first author would like to thank his parents Late Sri B. K. Chakraborty and Late Smt. Parul Chakraborty for their blessings. Further, he would like to thank and appreciate his wife Shewli and daughters Shreyati and Susprihaa for their love, support and inspiration throughout this project.

The second author would like to express his profound sense of gratitude towards his family members, especially his parents Sh. Naresh Prasad Jeswal and Smt. Prativa Jeswal and his sisters Pami, Sami and Nimi for their continuous support and blessings. Further, the second author greatly acknowledges the efforts of the first author for his continuous guidance, supervision and constant encouragement to carry out the present work without which this book would not have been possible.

Finally, the constructive suggestions and appreciations of the reviewers are sincerely acknowledged. Both the authors would also like to thank the NIT Rourkela authorities for moral and other support. And last but not least, the authors express their appreciation for the whole team at World Scientific Publishers who supported and worked with us throughout this project to ensure a smooth publication.

1

ANN Preliminaries

This chapter deals with the preliminaries related to Artificial Neural Network (ANN). Accordingly, different ANN architectures, learning rules along with activation functions have been discussed in detail.

1.1 Introduction

At the turn of the twenty first century, human life has greatly been influenced by different soft computing or artificial intelligence (AI) techniques. Different researchers have been working towards developing various novel AI technologies because of the growing demands from different sectors. Some of the AI techniques include Artificial Neural Network (ANN) or Connectionist systems, Support Vector Machine (SVM), Genetic Algorithm (GA), Swarm Intelligence, fuzzy and rough set theory, etc. ANN is one of the rapidly growing research areas of AI which has seen great development over the years. After the development of the back propagation algorithm in the late 1980s, various problems can be handled using ANN, which may sometimes be difficult to solve using the usual or known methods. Different applications of ANN can be seen in various fields such as function approximation, image processing, weather forecasting, robotics, medical diagnosis, data mining, speech and pattern recognition, traveling salesman problem, etc. and many more engineering and mathematical problems.

The concept of ANN has been inspired by the biological neural system [1]. The working principle of ANN resembles that of the human brain where several neurons (approximately 10^{11}) are interconnected and perform certain tasks from their own experiences. The concept of a computational model for ANN known as threshold logic has been developed by McCulloch and Pitts [2]. Rosenblatt [3] proposed an algorithm popularly coined as perceptron.

ANN comprises small identical units usually known as artificial neurons, which are analogous to the biological neurons. Each neuron has

1

been interconnected to each other using some connections. ANN has been designed using parallel-interconnected neurons. The connections have been assigned with some quantity known as weights. Generally, the ANN comprises three layers, namely input, hidden and output. The input layer interfaces with the external environment that fetches input patterns to the ANN model. The hidden layer is the intermediate layer between the input and output layers. There may be more than one hidden layer. Various methods have been proposed for calculating the number of hidden layers, but none of them have provided the exact formula to date. The output layer gathers and transfers the information as modeled to give.

Each neuron in the input layer receives inputs and processes it with the chosen weights following which the weighted sum can be passed through some activation function to give the final ANN output. Further, the error term is calculated using the ANN and target output. After calculating the error term, the weights get updated using different learning rules. Further, the procedure continues till the desired result has been achieved or the error has been minimized.

The concept of ANN has various advantages. In accordance with this, ANN may be used to find the solution of problems where the classical methods proved to be difficult or failed very often. The ANN model learns from examples or its own experiences so there is no need for it to be programmed explicitly. ANN learns quickly and very fast in solving various problems. It is an important tool in handling big data. ANN can work with partial or incomplete information. It can perform different tasks at the same time.

A single-layer ANN model has been depicted in Fig. 1.1.

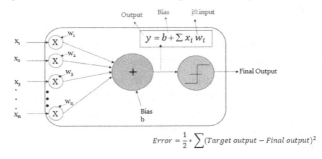

Fig. 1.1. Single-layer ANN model.

1.2 ANN Architectures [1, 9, 10]

Various ANN architectures have been developed so far based on the interconnection between the neurons and different layers. Some of the commonly used ANN architectures have been discussed further.

1. Feedforward Neural Network: The information flow is unidirectional or information passes through a feedforward manner in this network. Moreover, information flows from nth layer to $(n+1)$th layer, but not vice versa. Figure 1.2 shows the model of feedforward neural network.

   (a) Single-layer ANN architecture: It possesses a simple architecture without having hidden layers.
   (b) Multi-layer ANN architecture: It may comprise multiple hidden layers between the input and output layers.
   (c) Convolution Neural Network (CNN): It is a class of deep neural networks mainly used to analyze images. Further, CNN uses convolution instead of matrix multiplication in one of the layers.

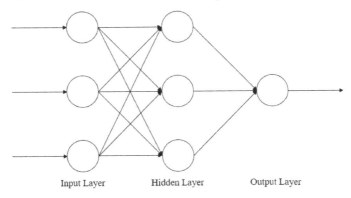

Fig. 1.2. Feedforward Neural Network

2. Feedback or Recurrent Neural Network (RcNN): RcNN comprises complex architectures with one or more than one hidden layer. In this model, information flow is possible both ways. Information passes from input to hidden and hidden to output layer and feeds back the information in a reverse manner. The model of feedback neural network has been depicted in Fig. 1.3.

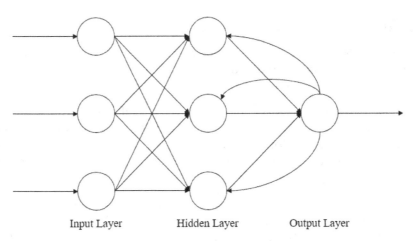

Input Layer   Hidden Layer   Output Layer

Fig. 1.3. Feedback Neural Network.

1.3 Learning Rules

The main aim of machine intelligence or AI is to make a machine intelligent. The main factor to make a machine intelligent is that it should be able learn itself from its experiences or by examples. Learning in ANN is broadly divided into three types viz.

(a) Supervised (learning with a supervisor)
(b) Unsupervised (learning without a supervisor)
(c) Reinforcement learning

In case of supervised learning, both input and target output are known, but on the other hand, the target output is unknown in unsupervised learning. Reinforcement learning is policy-based learning depending on rewards and penalties. For example, in case of a match, we get a positive or negative point, after that a policy is made to improve the game based on the rewards or penalty. In reinforcement learning, the Q-learning algorithm is used in general.

Learning rules assist the ANN models to update the weights and improve the performance of the ANN models. Learning rules may vary depending on the different ANN models as discussed in Section 1.2. The most used learning rules [1, 14, 20] have been listed as follows.

(i)   Hebbian Learning Rule

(ii)   Perceptron Learning Rule

(iii) Delta Learning Rule or Backpropagation Algorithm

(iv)   Winner-take-all Learning Rule

(v)   Correlation Learning Rule

(vi)   Outstar Learning Rule

Although different learning rules are presented, only the delta learning rule has been discussed in detail.

1.3.1 Backpropagation Algorithm or Delta Learning Rule [1, 9, 15]

Backpropagation algorithm is the backbone of ANN. After the evolution of backpropagation algorithm, ANN has seen great development over the years. Werbos [4] proposed the error backpropagation algorithm in his Ph.D. dissertation in the 1970s. Further, backpropagation algorithm was rediscovered by Rumelhart *et al.* [5] in 1986. It was also coined as the delta learning rule. Delta learning rule has been used in both supervised and unsupervised learning. Backpropagation network learns slowly and takes thousands of epochs (or iterations) to get the desired result.

An ANN architecture has been proposed with two input nodes x_i ($i = 1,2$), three hidden nodes z_j ($j = 1,2,3$) and two output nodes y_k ($k = 1,2$), which is shown in Fig. 1.4. Based on Fig. 1.4, the backpropagation algorithm has been addressed systematically.

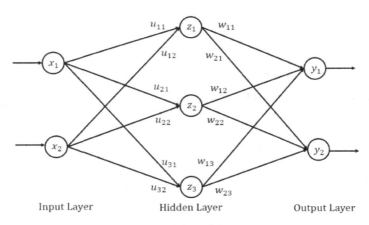

Fig. 1.4. ANN architecture.

Step 1: Weights between input to hidden layer and hidden to output layer have been chosen as u_{ji} and w_{kj}, respectively. The learning parameter is given by η, where $\eta \in [0,1]$.

The error term is defined as $E_{\max}$. Initially choose the error $E = 0$.

Step 2: The outputs of hidden and output layers have been found as

$$z_j \leftarrow g\left(\sum_{i=1}^{2} u_{ji} x_i\right), \ j = 1,2,3$$

$$y_k \leftarrow g\left(\sum_{j=1}^{3} w_{kj} z_j\right), \ k = 1,2$$

where g is the transfer function.

Step 3: The error function is calculated as

$$E = E + \frac{1}{2}\sum_{k=1}^{2}(l_k - y_k)^2$$

where l_k, y_k are the desired and ANN output, respectively.

Step 4: The error signal of output and hidden layers can be defined as

$$\delta_{yk} = \left[(l_k - y_k) g' \left(\sum_{j=1}^{3} w_{kj} z_j \right) \right]$$

$$\delta_{zj} = \left[(1 - z_j) g \left(\sum_{i=1}^{2} u_{ji} x_i \right) \right] \delta_{yk} w_{kj}$$

Step 5: The error gradients can be computed as

$$\frac{\partial E}{\partial u_{ji}} = \delta_{zj} x_i , \text{ where } j = 1, 2, 3 \text{ and } i = 1, 2$$

$$\frac{\partial E}{\partial w_{kj}} = \delta_{yk} z_j , \text{ where } j = 1, 2, 3 \text{ and } k = 1, 2$$

Step 6: Gradient descent algorithm which has been used to adjust the weights from input to hidden and hidden to output layers can be formulated as

$$u_{ji}^{t+1} = u_{ji}^{t} + \Delta u_{ji}^{t} = u_{ji}^{t} - \eta \frac{\partial E}{\partial u_{ji}^{t}}$$

$$w_{kj}^{t+1} = w_{kj}^{t} + \Delta w_{kj}^{t} = w_{kj}^{t} - \eta \frac{\partial E}{\partial w_{kj}^{t}}$$

where t is the iteration number.

Step 7: If $E = E_{max}$, truncate the process; else go to Step 2 and repeat the procedure.

1.4 Activation Function (or Transfer Function)

The activation function or transfer function [1, 14, 21, 23] are mathematical functions that can be applied to the weighted sum to get the final ANN output. Some commonly used activation functions are as follows.

    I.   Identity function
   II. Sigmoid function

      (i) Unipolar sigmoid function
     (ii) Bipolar sigmoid function

  III. Binary step function
  IV. Tanh function
   V. Rectified Linear Unit (ReLU)
  VI. Softmax function

Different activation functions have been listed, but only sigmoid and tangent hyperbolic function have been discussed in detail.

1.4.1 Sigmoid Function

It is an S-shaped strictly increasing and differentiable function, which is broadly divided into two types based on their outputs viz. unipolar and bipolar sigmoid functions.

(i) Unipolar sigmoid function

The unipolar sigmoid function may be defined as

$$\phi(t) = \frac{1}{1 + e^{-t}}$$

The output of unipolar sigmoid function can be ranged between $[0,1]$.

(ii) Bipolar sigmoid function

The bipolar sigmoidal function is given by

$$\phi(t) = -1 + \frac{2}{1 + e^{-t}}$$

The output of bipolar sigmoidal function lies within $[-1,1]$.

1.4.2 Tanh Function

The tanh function can be formulated as

$$\phi(t) = \frac{e^{-t} - e^{-t}}{e^{-t} + e^{-t}}$$

Figure 1.5 shows the plot of the tangent hyperbolic function. The output lies between [−1,1].

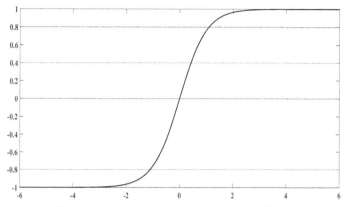

Fig. 1.5. Tangent hyperbolic function.

Finally, more details related to ANN preliminaries can be found in some standard books on neural networks [6–23].

1.5 Conclusion

The development of AI techniques has lead to various novel areas of research. The growing demand for it has led to the exploration of different aspects. Deep neural network is one such example of ANN. ANN is a novel technique in handling problems starting from healthcare to different industries due to its powerful learning and problem-solving capacity. Various data scientists have started to develop an improved ANN model with better learning ability.

References

[1] J. M. Zurada, (1992). Introduction to artificial neural systems. West publishing company, St. Paul.

[2] W. S. McCulloch and W. Pitts, (1943). A logical calculus of the ideas immanent in nervous activity. *The Bulletin of Mathematical Biophysics*, 5(4), 115–133.

[3] F. Rosenblatt, (1958). The perceptron: A probabilistic model for information storage and organization in the brain. *Psychological Review, 65*(6), 386.

[4] P. Werbos, (1974). Beyond Regression: New Tools for Prediction and Analysis in the Behavioral Sciences. Ph. D. dissertation, Harvard University.

[5] D. E. Rumelhart, G. E. Hinton, and R. J. Williams, (1986). Parallel Distributed Processing. MIT press, Cambridge, MA.

[6] H. White, (1992). *Artificial neural networks: Approximation and learning theory*. Blackwell Publishers, Inc.

[7] D. Livingstone, (2008). *Artificial neural networks: Methods and applications*. Humana Press, Totowa, NJ.

[8] P. J. Braspenning, F. Thuijsman and A. J. M. M. Weijters, (1995). Artificial neural networks: An introduction to ANN theory and practice. Springer Science & Business Media.

[9] S. S. Haykin, (2009). *Neural networks and learning machines*. Prentice Hall, New York.

[10] M. H. Hassoun, (1995). *Fundamentals of artificial neural networks*. MIT press.

[11] K. Gurney, (2014). *An introduction to neural networks*. CRC press.

[12] M. Anthony and P. L. Bartlett, (2009). *Neural network learning: Theoretical foundations*. Cambridge university press.

[13] B. Müller, J. Reinhardt and M. T. Strickland, (2012). *Neural networks: An introduction*. Springer Science & Business Media.

[14] S. Chakraverty and S. Mall (2017). Artificial neural networks for engineers and scientists: Solving ordinary differential equations. CRC Press.

[15] S. Chakraverty, D. M. Sahoo, and N. R. Mahato, (2019). Concepts of Soft Computing: Fuzzy and ANN with Programming. Springer.

[16] P. De Wilde, (1996). *Neural network models: An analysis*. Heidelberg: Springer.

[17] A. Browne (Ed.). (1997). *Neural network analysis, architectures and applications*. CRC Press.

[18] R. M. Golden, and R. Golden, (1996). *Mathematical methods for neural network analysis and design*. MIT Press.

[19] M. T. Hagan, H. B. Demuth, and M. Beale, (1997). *Neural network design*. PWS Publishing Co.

[20] R. Rojas, (2013). *Neural networks: A systematic introduction*. Springer Science & Business Media.

[21] L. V. Fausett, (2006). *Fundamentals of neural networks: Architectures, algorithms and applications*. Pearson Education India.

[22] J. A. Freeman, and D. M. Skapura, (1991). *Neural networks: Algorithms, applications, and programming techniques*. Addison Wesley Longman Publishing Co., Inc.

[23] B. Yegnanarayana, (2009). *Artificial neural networks*. PHI Learning Pvt. Ltd.

2

Mathematical Preliminaries

This chapter addresses the basic definitions of polynomial, transcendental and Diophantine equations. Further, the concept of linear and nonlinear systems of equations have been defined. And finally, a brief idea of linear and nonlinear eigenvalue problems has also been incorporated.

2.1 Introduction

An equation may be expressed as the combination of two expressions having an equality sign. Finding the solution of an equation is to find the value of unknown variables for which equality will always be true. Each side of the equation contains one or more than one term. These equations may be both linear and nonlinear. One may come across different types of equations while solving various engineering and science problems. These equations may be of various types such as polynomial, algebraic, transcendental, Diophantine, linear/nonlinear system of equations and eigenvalue problems, etc.

Further, the aforementioned equations/problems have been discussed in detail.

2.2 Polynomial Equations [1–5]

Polynomial or algebraic equation can be defined as

$$P_n(x) = 0$$

$$\text{or, } P_n(x) \equiv p_n x^n + p_{n-1} x^{n-1} + \cdots + p_1 x + p_o = 0 \qquad (2.1)$$

where $P_n(x)$ is a polynomial with different coefficients $p_n, p_{n-1}, \cdots, p_1, p_o$ defined over the field of R and x is the unknown variable.

Some examples of polynomial equations are as follows:

- $x^3 - x^2 + 2x + 1 = 0$
- $x^2 - 2x = 5$
- $x^4 - 4x^2 - 8x = 2$

2.3 Transcendental Equations [1–5]

An equation involving different transcendental functions viz. exponential, logarithmic, trigonometric, etc. is said to be a transcendental equation.

General model of a transcendental equation may be defined as

$$a_1 e^x + a_2 \log x + \cdots + a_n \sin x = a_0 \tag{2.2}$$

where, $a_1, a_2, \cdots, a_n$ are the different coefficients, $e^x, \log x, \sin x$ are the different transcendental functions and a_0 is the constant term.

A few examples of transcendental equations are as follows:

- $e^x - \tan x = 0$
- $\sin x - \pi^e = 1$
- $\ln x = e^2$

2.4 Diophantine Equations [6–10]

Diophantine equation is a form of polynomial equation having two or more unknown variables. In this case, we are only interested (here) in the integer solutions. The Diophantine equation may be written as

$$f(a_1, a_2, \cdots, a_n, x_1, x_2, \cdots, x_n) = d \tag{2.3}$$

where $a_1, a_2, \cdots, a_n$ are the different coefficients, $x_1, x_2, \cdots, x_n$ are the unknown variables and d is an integer. Equation (2.3) has a solution if and only if gcd $(a_1, a_2, \cdots, a_n)$ divides d .

A few examples are as follows:

- $x_1^2 + x_2^2 = x_3^2$

- $x_1 + x_2 = 1$
- $2x_1 + 3x_2 = 6$

2.5 Linear System of Equations (LSEs) [11–15]

A linear system can be defined as the collection of two or more linear equations. A set of m linear equations with n variables can be formulated as

$$A_{11}x_1 + A_{12}x_2 + \cdots + A_{1n}x_n = B_1$$

$$A_{21}x_1 + A_{22}x_2 + \cdots + A_{2n}x_n = B_2 \qquad (2.4)$$

$$\vdots$$

$$A_{n1}x_1 + A_{n2}x_2 + \cdots + A_{nm}x_n = B_n$$

where $x_1, x_2, \cdots, x_n$ are unknown variables, $A_{11}, A_{12}, \cdots, A_{nm}$ are coefficients and $B_1, B_2, \cdots, B_n$ are the constant terms.

For example,

- $2x_1 + 7x_2 + 4x_3 = 0$
  $x_1 - x_2 + 6x_3 = 0$
  $4x_1 + 3x_2 + x_3 = 0$
- $x_1 + 3x_2 - 8x_3 = 10$
  $-10x_1 + 6x_2 + 5x_3 - 8x_4 = 6$
  $6x_1 - 3x_2 + x_3 - x_4 = 8$
  $4x_1 - 7x_2 + x_3 + 2x_4 = 8$

The system (2.4) is said to be homogeneous if the constant terms are equal to zero, otherwise it is nonhomogeneous.

LSEs may have broadly three types of solution sets viz.
   (1) The system has a unique solution.
   (2) The system has infinitely many solutions.
   (3) The system has no solution.

Moreover, an LSE is consistent if the system possesses at least one solution; on the contrary, it is inconsistent if there is no solution.

2.6 Systems of Nonlinear Equations [11–15]

A nonlinear system is a combination of two or more nonlinear equations. A nonlinear system may be defined as

$$f_1(x_1, x_2, \cdots, x_n) = d_1$$

$$f_2(x_1, x_2, \cdots, x_n) = d_2 \qquad (2.5)$$

$$\vdots$$

$$f_n(x_1, x_2, \cdots, x_n) = d_n$$

where x_i $(i = 1, 2, \cdots, n)$ are unknown variables, f_i $(i = 1, 2, \cdots, n)$ are nonlinear real functions of x_i and d_i $(i = 1, 2, \cdots, n)$ are the constant terms.

Some examples of nonlinear systems are as follows:

- $x^2 + y^3 = 3$
  $2x + 3y^2 = 1$

- $2x^2 + y^3 + 3z = 3$
  $x + 3y^2 = 1$
  $y - \tan z = 2$

2.7 Eigenvalue Problems [11–13]

Eigenvalue problems have also arisen in various circumstances. In general, the eigenvalue problem may be of two types viz. linear and nonlinear.

Given a matrix A of dimension $m \times m$, find a scalar λ and a non-zero vector x such that

$$Ax = \lambda x$$

where λ is the eigenvalue and x is the corresponding eigenvector. The eigenvalues may be both real and complex.

2.8 Nonlinear Eigenvalue Problem (NEP)

NEP [16–19] is a generalization of the linear eigenvalue problem. The NEP may be of different types depending upon the degree of the eigenvalue such as quadratic, cubic, etc. Quadratic eigenvalue problems [20–22] and cubic eigenvalue problems [23] are the special cases of NEP. Till date, very few methods have been proposed to handle these problems.

NEP may be defined as

$$A(\lambda)x = 0 \tag{2.6}$$

where λ is the eigenvalue and x is the eigenvector corresponding to the eigenvalue λ. Further, $A(\lambda)$ is the matrix-valued nonlinear function of λ. The general form of NEP (2.6) having degree n is written as follows:

$$A(\lambda)x = \sum_{i=0}^{n} \lambda^i A_i x = (A_0 + A_1\lambda + \cdots\cdots + A_{n-1}\lambda^{n-1} + A_n\lambda^n)x = 0 \tag{2.7}$$

where the coefficients A_i ($i = 0, 1, \cdots, n$) are square matrices.

Depending upon the degree of λ, there exist different forms of NEPs such as

- Quadratic eigenvalue problem
  ($A(\lambda)x = (A_0 + A_1\lambda + A_2\lambda^2)x = 0$)
- Cubic eigenvalue problem
  ($A(\lambda)x = (A_0 + A_1\lambda + A_2\lambda^2 + A_3\lambda^3)x = 0$), etc.

References

[1] C. F. Gerald, (2004). *Applied numerical analysis.* Pearson Education India.

[2] K. E. Atkinson, (2008). *An introduction to numerical analysis.* John Wiley & Sons.

[3] R. B. Bhat and S. Chakraverty (2004). *Numerical analysis in engineering.* Alpha Science Int'l Ltd.

[4] S. D. Conte and C. De Boor (2017). *Elementary numerical analysis: An algorithmic approach*. Society for Industrial and Applied Mathematics.

[5] W. Gautschi, (1997). *Numerical analysis*. Springer Science & Business Media.

[6] D. M. Burton, (2006). *Elementary number theory*. Tata McGraw-Hill Education.

[7] K. H. Rosen, (2011). *Elementary number theory*. Pearson Education.

[8] T. Koshy, (2002). *Elementary number theory with applications*. Academic press.

[9] T. M. Apostol, (2013). *Introduction to analytic number theory*. Springer Science & Business Media.

[10] H. Rademacher, (2012). *Topics in analytic number theory* (Vol. 169). Springer Science & Business Media.

[11] K. Hoffman and R. Kunze (1971) Linear algebra. Englewood Cliffs, New Jersey.

[12] G. Strang,(1993). Introduction to linear algebra. Wellesley, MA: Wellesley-Cambridge Press.

[13] L. Hogben, (2013). Handbook of linear algebra. Chapman and Hall/CRC.

[14] H. Anton and C. Rorres (2013). *Elementary linear algebra: Applications version*. John Wiley & Sons.

[15] O. Bretscher, (1997). *Linear algebra with applications*. Eaglewood Cliffs, NJ: Prentice Hall.

[16] P. Guillaume, (1999). Nonlinear eigenproblems. *SIAM Journal on Matrix Analysis and Applications*, *20*(3), 575–595.

[17] J. Henderson and H. Wang, (1997). Positive solutions for nonlinear eigenvalue problems. *Journal of Mathematical Analysis and Applications*, *208*(1), 252–259.

[18] P. Lindqvist, (2008). A nonlinear eigenvalue problem. *Topics in Mathematical Analysis*, *3*, 175–203.

[19] H. Voß (2004). An Arnoldi method for nonlinear eigenvalue problems. *BIT Numerical Mathematics*, *44*(2), 387–401.

[20] F. Tisseur and K. Meerbergen, (2001). The quadratic eigenvalue problem. *SIAM Review*, *43*(2), 235–286.

[21] Z. Bai and Y. Su, (2005). SOAR: A second-order Arnoldi method for the solution of the quadratic eigenvalue problem. *SIAM Journal on Matrix Analysis and Applications*, *26*(3), 640–659.

[22] S. Hammarling, C. J. Munro, and F. Tisseur, (2013). An algorithm for the complete solution of quadratic eigenvalue problems. *ACM Transactions on Mathematical Software (TOMS)*, *39*(3), 1–19.

[23] T. M. Hwang, W. W. Lin, J. L. Liu, and W. Wang, (2005). Jacobi–Davidson methods for cubic eigenvalue problems. *Numerical Linear Algebra with Applications*, *12*(7), 605–624.

3

Polynomial Equations with Application in Solving Bakery problem

This chapter introduces an ANN-based technique for solving polynomial equations. A four-layer architecture with detailed procedure has been included for handling these equations. Various examples and an application of bakery problem have been solved to show the efficacy of the developed ANN method.

3.1 Introduction

Polynomial equation is an important concept in mathematical sciences. Many engineering and science problems may be transferred to polynomial equations. Although different traditional numerical methods exist to handle polynomial equations, these methods may sometimes be unconducive to handle polynomial equations having higher degrees. In this scenario, ANN may be a useful/alternative technique to handle these equations. Polynomial equations have various applications in different fields such as projectile motion, bakery problem, Pythagorean theorem and curve fitting, etc.

Different techniques have been developed to handle polynomial equations. In this regard, various traditional numerical methods may be found in [1–9]. Pan [10] has written a survey paper discussing different algorithmic approaches and their computational costs for solving polynomial equations. A unified method for solving polynomial equations of degree less than five have been proposed by Kulkarni [11].

3.2 General Model of a Polynomial Equation

A general model of a polynomial equation may be defined as

$$P_n(x) = 0$$

$$\text{Or, } P_n(x) \equiv p_1 x + p_2 x^2 + \cdots + p_n x^n = p_0 \tag{3.1}$$

where $P_n(x)$ is a polynomial with different coefficients $p_1, p_2, \cdots, p_n, p_0$ is the constant term and x is the unknown variable.

3.2.1 ANN Procedure for Solving Polynomial Equation

A detailed ANN model for solving Eq. (3.1) is depicted in Fig. 3.1.

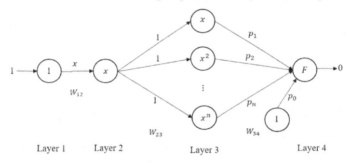

Fig. 3.1. Multi-layer ANN architecture for Eq. (3.1).

Generalized architecture for solving a polynomial equation is shown in Fig. 3.1, which comprises of four layers, that is Layer 1 (input layer), Layers 2 and 3 (hidden layers) and Layer 4 (output layer). The input layer consists of one linear unit node with a constant input equal to unity. Further, first hidden layer (Layer 2) has one node for the linear term x and Layer 3 comprises of a number of nodes depending upon the polynomial equation. Finally, output layer consists of summation units whose total input is the expression of the left-hand side of Eq. (3.1). It may be seen in Fig. 3.1 that weights from Layer 2 to Layer 3 are fixed, that is unity. Different coefficients of the Eq. (3.1) are considered as the weights between Layers 3 and 4. There is only variable weight joining Layer 1 to 2, which is the solution of the given Eq. (3.1). There is also a bias node connecting to the output node and W_{ij} denotes the weights between the layers i and j. Further, the weights are written in matrix form as follows:

$$W_{12} = \left[W_{12}^{(1)} \right] = [x]$$

$$W_{23} = \begin{bmatrix} W_{23}^{(11)} \\ W_{23}^{(21)} \\ \vdots \\ W_{23}^{(nl)} \end{bmatrix} = \begin{bmatrix} 1 \\ 1 \\ \vdots \\ 1 \end{bmatrix}$$

$$W_{34} = \begin{bmatrix} W_{34}^{(11)} \\ W_{34}^{(21)} \\ \vdots \\ W_{34}^{(nl)} \end{bmatrix} = \begin{bmatrix} P_1 \\ P_2 \\ \vdots \\ P_n \end{bmatrix}$$

where the subscripts 1, 2, 3, 4 denote the different layers of the ANN model.

The input–output relationship of the network architecture of the neurons is given by $u_k = f(U_k)$ ($k = 2,3,4$), where U is the input to the neuron, f is its activation function and u is the produced output. The inputs with vector notation of different layers are written as

$$U_2 = [U_2^{(1)}] = [x]$$

$$U_3 = [U_3^{(1)} \quad U_3^{(2)} \quad \cdots \quad U_3^{(n)}] = [x \quad x \quad \cdots \quad x]$$

$$U_4 = [U_4^{(1)}] = [F(x)]$$

Using the activation functions for Layer 2 (Identity function), Layer 3 (Polynomial function) and Layer 4 (Tangent hyperbolic function) as follows:

$$f_2 = [f_2^{(1)}(U)] = [U]$$

$$f_3 = [f_3^{(1)}(U) \quad f_3^{(2)}(U) \quad \cdots \quad f_3^{(n)}(U)] = [U \quad U^2 \quad \cdots \quad U^n]$$

$$f_4 = [f_4^{(1)}(U)] = [\tanh(U)]$$

their corresponding outputs can be computed thus:

$$u_2 = [u_2^{(1)}] = [x]$$

$$u_3 = [u_3^{(1)} \quad u_3^{(2)} \quad \cdots \quad u_3^{(n)}] = [x \quad x^2 \quad \cdots \quad x^n]$$

$$u_4 = [u_4^{(1)}] = [\tanh[F(x)]]$$

The well-known backpropagation algorithm is applied to solve the titled problem. As such, the forward and backward pass with weight update formula has been discussed further.

Forward Pass:

Using the backpropagation algorithm, the network input to the jth hidden neuron of any hidden layer is given by

$$net_j = \sum_{i=1}^{n} W_{ij} x_i + b_j$$

where W_{ij} is the weight from the input unit to the hidden unit, x_i is the input vector and b_j is the bias. Output of jth hidden neuron can be computed as

$$y_j = f(net_j)$$

where f is the activation function.

This concept may be used for the network and notations discussed in the previous section can be expressed as follows:

The input to the neurons of Layer 2 is written as

$$U_2^{(1)} = W_{12}^{(1)}$$

and the corresponding output is given by

$$u_2^{(1)} = f_2^{(1)}(U_2^{(1)}) = x$$

Layer 3 consists of n units corresponding to the values $i = 1, 2, \cdots, n$. The inputs to the n units are given as

$$U_3^{(i)} = W_{23}^{(1i)} u_2^{(1)} \tag{3.2}$$

The outputs of Layer 3 can be found as

$$u_3^{(1)} = f_3^{(1)}(U_3^{(1)}) = x$$

$$u_3^{(2)} = f_3^{(2)}(U_3^{(2)}) = x^2$$

$$\vdots$$

$$u_3^{(n)} = f_3^{(n)}(U_3^{(n)}) = x^n$$

The input to the linear neurons of Layer 4 is calculated as

$$U_4^{(1)} = \sum_{j=1}^{n} W_{34}^{(j1)} u_3^{(j)} - p_0 = F(x) \tag{3.3}$$

and the corresponding output is calculated as

$$U_4^{(1)} \equiv o = \tanh(U_4^{(1)}) = \tanh[F(x)] \tag{3.4}$$

Backward Pass:

The different parameters in case of backward pass for Layers 2, 3 and 4 are defined as

$$\gamma_2 = [\gamma_2^{(1)}]$$

$$\gamma_3 = [\gamma_3^{(1)} \quad \gamma_3^{(2)} \quad \cdots \quad \gamma_3^{(n)}]$$

$$\gamma_4 = [\gamma_4^{(1)}]$$

Starting with the output layer and the ANN, output is of the form

$$o = \tanh[F(x)]$$

and the corresponding desired output is chosen as $h = 0$ while the activation function for Layer 4 is chosen to be a hyperbolic tangent function whose derivative is

$$\tanh'(x) = 1 - \tanh^2(x)$$

Then the element of γ_4 is estimated as

$$\gamma_4^{(1)} = (h-o)\tanh'(U_4^{(1)}) = -\tanh[F(x)](1-\tanh^2[F(x)])$$

Further using the γ_4 value, the γ values of Layer 3 have been calculated as

$$\gamma_3^{(i)} = (W_{34}^{(i1)}\gamma_4^{(1)}) \cdot (f_3^{(i)'}(U_3^{(i)})), \text{ where } i = 1, 2, \cdots, n \tag{3.5}$$

and the different derivatives involved in Eq. (3.5) can be computed as
$$f_3^{(1)'}(U_3^{(1)}) = 1, f_3^{(2)'}(U_3^{(2)}) = 2x, \cdots, f_3^{(n)'}(U_3^{(n)}) = nx^{n-1}.$$

Further, Eq. (3.5) is rewritten as

$$\gamma_3^{(1)} = (W_{34}^{(11)}\gamma_3^{(n)})(1) = [-f(F)(1-f^2(F))](1)$$

$$\gamma_3^{(2)} = (W_{34}^{(21)}\gamma_4^{(1)})(2x) = [-f(F)(1-f^2(F))](2x)$$

$$\vdots$$

$$\gamma_3^{(n)} = (W_{34}^{(n1)}\gamma_3^{(n)})(nx^{n-1}) = [-f(F)(1-f^2(F))](nx^{n-1})$$

Finally, the γ value of Layer 2 is estimated using the γ_3 values computed in Eq. (3.5).

$$\gamma_2^{(1)} = \left(\sum_{j=1}^{n} W_{23}^{(j1)}\gamma_3^{(j)}\right) \cdot (f_2^{(1)'}(U_2^{(1)})) \tag{3.6}$$

where the derivative involved in Eq. (3.6) is equal to $f_2^{(1)'}(U_2^{(1)}) = 1$. As such, Eq. (3.6) is rewritten in the following form:

$$\gamma_2^{(1)} = W_{23}^{(11)}\gamma_3^{(1)} + W_{23}^{(21)}\gamma_3^{(2)} + \cdots + W_{23}^{(n1)}\gamma_3^{(n)} = \gamma_4^{(1)}\frac{\partial F(x)}{\partial x}$$

Updating weights of the network architecture:

Using the backpropagation algorithm, the weight updating equation is given by

$$W_{12}^{(1)} = W_{12}^{(1)} + \eta\gamma_2^{(1)} = W_{12}^{(1)} + \eta\gamma_4^{(1)} \frac{\partial F(x)}{\partial W_{12}^{(1)}} \qquad (3.7)$$

where η is the learning parameter.

The mean square error for the model is calculated as

$$E = \frac{1}{2}(h-o)^2 = \frac{1}{2}f^2[F(x)] \qquad (3.8)$$

Differentiating Eq. (3.8) with respect to $W_{12}^{(1)}$, we have

$$\frac{\partial E}{\partial W_{12}^{(1)}} = -f(F(x))(1 - f^2(F(x)))\frac{\partial F(x)}{\partial W_{12}^{(1)}} = -\gamma_4^{(1)}\frac{\partial F(x)}{\partial W_{12}^{(1)}} \qquad (3.9)$$

Finally, the weight update equation is

$$W_{12}^{(1)} = W_{12}^{(1)} - \eta\frac{\partial E}{\partial W_{12}^{(1)}} \qquad (3.10)$$

3.3 Numerical Examples

Four examples of polynomial equations have been solved in this section using the proposed ANN procedure. Further, detailed ANN architecture with few steps in case of example 3.1 has been given. Convergence tables and/or plots for the solutions have also been included.

Example 3.1: Let us consider a polynomial equation

$$x^3 - 6x^2 + 4x + 4 = 0 \qquad (3.11)$$

which has roots as -0.5341, 1.4827 and 5.0514.

The proposed ANN procedure has been applied to solve Eq. (3.11). The network architecture for solving Eq. (3.11) has been constructed in Fig. 3.2. The detailed procedure for solving polynomial equation has been presented already in Section 3.2.1. However, a few steps of the ANN procedure are discussed for this example for clear understanding.

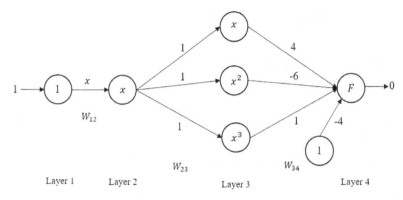

Fig. 3.2. ANN architecture for Eq. (3.11).

As seen in Fig. 3.2, the ANN architecture comprises four layers. The input layer consists of one linear unit node with a constant input equal to unity. Further, Layer 2 has one node for the linear term x and Layer 3 comprises a number of nodes depending upon Eq. (3.11). Finally, Layer 4 consists of summation units whose total input is the expression of the left-hand side of Eq. (3.11). It may be seen in Fig. 3.2 that weights from Layer 2 to Layer 3 are fixed, that is unity. Different coefficients of the Eq. (3.11) are considered as the weights between Layers 3 and 4. There is only variable weight joining Layer 1 to 2, which is the solution of the given Eq. (3.11). There is also a bias node connecting to the output node.

The weights for different layers are written as follows:

$$W_{12} = [W_{12}^{(1)}] = [x]$$

$$W_{23} = \begin{bmatrix} W_{23}^{(11)} \\ W_{23}^{(21)} \\ W_{23}^{(31)} \end{bmatrix} = \begin{bmatrix} 1 \\ 1 \\ 1 \end{bmatrix}$$

$$W_{23} = \begin{bmatrix} W_{34}^{(11)} \\ W_{34}^{(21)} \\ W_{34}^{(31)} \end{bmatrix} = \begin{bmatrix} 4 \\ -6 \\ 1 \end{bmatrix}$$

The input–output relationship of the network architecture of the neurons is given by $u_k = f(U_k)$ ($k = 2,3,4$), where U is the input to the neuron, f is its activation function and u is the produced output. The inputs with vector notations of different layers are written as

$$U_2 = [U_2^{(1)}] = [x]$$

$$U_3 = [U_3^{(1)} \quad U_3^{(2)} \quad U_3^{(3)}] = [x \quad x \quad x]$$

$$U_4 = [U_4^{(1)}] = [F(x)]$$

Using the activation functions for Layer 2 (Identity function), Layer 3 (Polynomial function) and Layer 4 (Tangent hyperbolic function) as follows:

$$f_2 = [f_2^{(1)}(U)]$$

$$f_3 = [f_3^{(1)}(U) \quad f_3^{(2)}(U) \quad f_3^{(3)}(U)]$$

$$f_4 = [f_4^{(1)}(U)]$$

and their corresponding outputs can be computed thus:

$$u_2 = [u_2^{(1)}] = [x]$$

$$u_3 = [u_3^{(1)} \quad u_3^{(2)} \quad u_3^{(3)}] = [x \quad x^2 \quad x^3]$$

$$u_4 = [u_4^{(1)}] = [\tanh[F(x)]]$$

Accordingly, the ANN procedure is applied to get the desired solutions. The initial weights (guesses) have been arbitrarily chosen as 0.1, 0.8 and 4 to get the first (-0.5341), second (1.4827) and third (5.0514) root of Eq. (3.11), respectively. Here, we have taken the learning parameter as 0.01 for computing all the three roots. As such, successive simulation results with respect to different stopping criteria and number of epochs for different roots have been included in Tables 3.1 to 3.3. Convergence plots of the roots have been depicted in Figs. 3.3 to 3.5.

Table 3.1. Convergence table for the first root of Eq. (3.11).

First Root	Stopping Criteria	Epoch
0.0881	< 0.5	2
-0.5088	< 0.1	52
-0.5253	$< 10^{-2}$	55
-0.5321	$< 10^{-3}$	59
-0.5335	$< 10^{-4}$	62
-0.5339	$< 10^{-5}$	65
-0.5340	$< 10^{-6}$	68
-0.5341	$< 10^{-7}$	71
-0.5341	$< 10^{-8}$	74
-0.5341	$< 10^{-9}$	77

Table 3.2. Convergence table for the second root of Eq. (3.11).

Second Root	Stopping Criteria	Epoch
0.8155	< 0.5	2
1.4385	< 0.1	42
1.4684	$< 10^{-2}$	46
1.4785	$< 10^{-3}$	50
1.4815	$< 10^{-4}$	54
1.4823	$< 10^{-5}$	58

1.4826	$<10^{-6}$	61
1.4827	$<10^{-7}$	65
1.4827	$<10^{-8}$	69
1.4827	$<10^{-9}$	73

Table 3.3. Convergence table for the third root of Eq. (3.11).

Third Root	Stopping Criteria	Epoch
4.0168	<0.5	2
5.0426	<0.1	63
5.0509	$<10^{-2}$	65
5.0509	$<10^{-2}$	65
5.0513	$<10^{-4}$	66
5.0514	$<10^{-5}$	67
5.0514	$<10^{-6}$	68
5.0514	$<10^{-7}$	68
5.0514	$<10^{-8}$	69

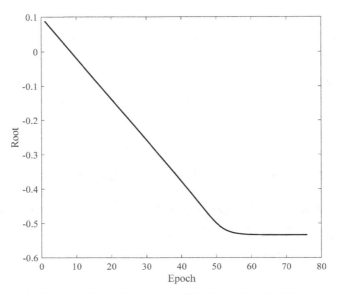

Fig. 3.3. First Root (-0.5341) of Eq. (3.11).

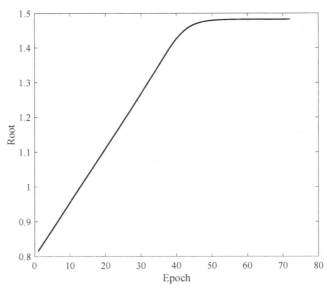

Fig. 3.4. Second Root (1.4827) of Eq. (3.11)

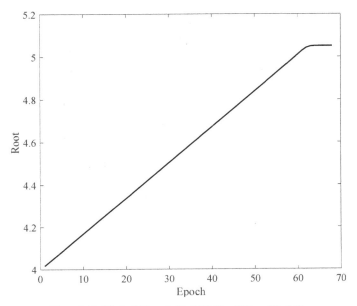

Fig. 3.5. Third Root (5.0514) of Eq. (3.11).

Example 3.2: A polynomial equation is used in this example

$$x^4 + 7x^3 + 11x^2 - 7x - 12 = 0 \tag{3.12}$$

which has roots as -4, -3, -1 and 1.

The ANN architecture for Eq. (3.12) has been constructed in Fig. 3.6.

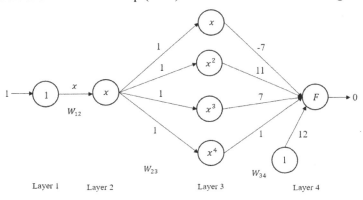

Fig. 3.6. ANN architecture for Eq. (3.12).

As such, the ANN method is applied to solve Eq. (3.12) for getting desired roots. In this case, initial weights have been selected as -6, -2, 0.1 and 0.4 to get the first (-4.0000), second (-3.0000), third (-1.0000) and fourth (1.0000) root of Eq. (3.12), respectively. The learning parameter is chosen as 0.001 (for first and third roots), 0.01 (for the second root) and 0.0001 (for the fourth root), respectively. Accordingly, simulation results for the solutions have been included in Tables 3.4 to 3.7. Convergence plots of roots have been shown in Figs. 3.7 to 3.10.

Table 3.4. Convergence table for the first root of Eq. (3.12).

First Root	Stopping Criteria	Epoch
-4.5514	<0.5	32
-4.0218	<0.1	76
-4.0061	$<10^{-2}$	81
-4.0022	$<10^{-3}$	85
-4.0006	$<10^{-4}$	90
-4.0002	$<10^{-5}$	94
-4.0001	$<10^{-6}$	99
-4.0000	$<10^{-7}$	103
-4.0000	$<10^{-8}$	108
-4.0000	$<10^{-9}$	112

Table 3.5. Convergence table for the second root of Eq. (3.12).

Second Root	Stopping Criteria	Epoch
-2.0042	<0.5	2
-2.9875	<0.1	54

-2.9955	$<10^{-2}$	55
-2.9984	$<10^{-3}$	56
-2.9994	$<10^{-4}$	57
-2.9999	$<10^{-5}$	59
-3.0000	$<10^{-6}$	60
-3.0000	$<10^{-7}$	61
-3.0000	$<10^{-8}$	62
-3.0000	$<10^{-9}$	63

Table 3.6. Convergence table for the third root of Eq. (3.12).

Third Root	Stopping Criteria	Epoch
0.0981	<0.5	2
-0.9684	<0.1	240
-0.9901	$<10^{-2}$	248
-0.9972	$<10^{-3}$	256
-0.9990	$<10^{-4}$	263
-0.9997	$<10^{-5}$	271
-0.9999	$<10^{-6}$	278
-1.0000	$<10^{-7}$	285
-1.0000	$<10^{-8}$	293
-1.0000	$<10^{-9}$	300

Table 3.7. Convergence table for the fourth root of Eq. (3.12).

Fourth Root	Stopping Criteria	Epoch
0.4002	< 0.5	2
0.9900	< 0.1	909
0.9971	$< 10^{-2}$	917
0.9991	$< 10^{-3}$	924
0.9997	$< 10^{-4}$	931
0.9999	$< 10^{-5}$	937
1.0000	$< 10^{-6}$	944
1.0000	$< 10^{-7}$	950
1.0000	$< 10^{-8}$	957
1.0000	$< 10^{-9}$	964

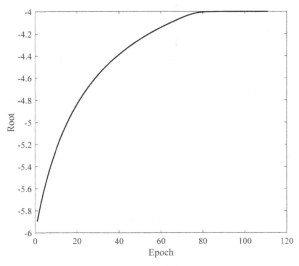

Fig. 3.7. First Root (-4.0000) of Eq. (3.12)

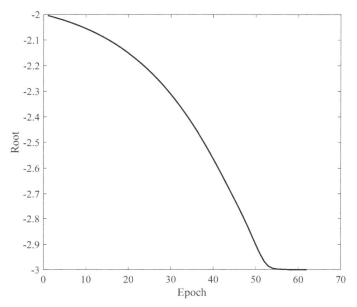

Fig. 3.8. Second Root (-3.0000) of Eq. (3.12).

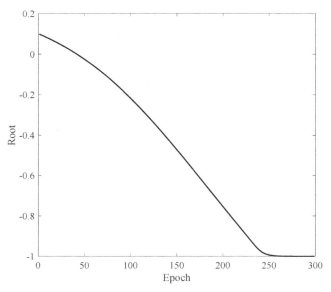

Fig. 3.9. Third Root (-1.0000) of Eq. (3.12)

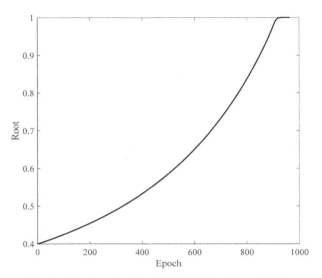

Fig. 3.10. Fourth Root (1.0000) of Eq. (3.12).

Example 3.3: The following polynomial equation is considered:

$$x^5 - 5x^4 + 5x^3 + 5x^2 - 6x - 1 = 0 \qquad (3.13)$$

which has roots as -0.9541, -0.1510, 1.2758, 1.7907 and 3.0385.

Equation (3.13) is solved using the ANN procedure. Initial weights are considered as -0.7, 0.2, 0.6, 1.6, 2.7 to obtain the final solutions as -0.9541, -0.1510, 1.2758, 1.7907, 3.0385, respectively. The learning parameter for computing first, second and fifth roots is 0.01 and for others, it is 0.1. Simulation result of different roots for Eq. (3.13) has been included in Tables 3.8 to 3.12. Further, Figs. 3.11 to 3.15 demonstrate the convergence plots of the roots.

Table 3.8. Convergence table for the first root of Eq. (3.13).

First Root	Stopping Criteria	Epoch
-0.7102	< 0.5	2
-0.9369	< 0.1	24

-0.9510	$<10^{-2}$	27
-0.9532	$<10^{-3}$	29
-0.9538	$<10^{-4}$	31
-0.9540	$<10^{-5}$	33
-0.9540	$<10^{-6}$	34
-0.9541	$<10^{-7}$	36
-0.9541	$<10^{-8}$	38
-0.9541	$<10^{-9}$	40

Table 3.9. Convergence table for the second root of Eq. (3.13).

Second Root	Stopping Criteria	Epoch
0.1848	<0.5	2
-0.1038	<0.1	21
-0.1386	$<10^{-2}$	26
-0.1471	$<10^{-3}$	30
-0.1498	$<10^{-4}$	34
-0.1506	$<10^{-5}$	38
-0.1509	$<10^{-6}$	42
-0.1509	$<10^{-7}$	46
-0.1510	$<10^{-8}$	50
-0.1510	$<10^{-9}$	54
-0.1510	$<10^{-10}$	58

Table 3.10. Convergence table for the third root of Eq. (3.13).

Third Root	Stopping Criteria	Epoch
0.6733	< 0.5	2
1.2334	< 0.1	10
1.2553	$< 10^{-2}$	11
1.2708	$< 10^{-3}$	13
1.2746	$< 10^{-4}$	15
1.2752	$< 10^{-5}$	16
1.2757	$< 10^{-6}$	18
1.2758	$< 10^{-7}$	20
1.2758	$< 10^{-8}$	21
1.2758	$< 10^{-9}$	23

Table 3.11. Convergence table for the fourth root of Eq. (3.13).

Fourth Root	Stopping Criteria	Epoch
1.6247	< 0.5	2
1.6247	< 0.1	2
1.7605	$< 10^{-2}$	10
1.7809	$< 10^{-3}$	14
1.7877	$< 10^{-4}$	18
1.7898	$< 10^{-5}$	22

1.7905	$<10^{-6}$	26
1.7906	$<10^{-7}$	30
1.7907	$<10^{-8}$	34
1.7907	$<10^{-9}$	38

Table 3.12. Convergence table for the fifth root of Eq. (3.13).

Fifth Root	Stopping Criteria	Epoch
2.7101	<0.5	2
3.0334	<0.1	34
3.0367	$<10^{-2}$	35
3.0383	$<10^{-3}$	37
3.0384	$<10^{-4}$	38
3.0385	$<10^{-5}$	39
3.0385	$<10^{-6}$	40
3.0385	$<10^{-7}$	41
3.0385	$<10^{-8}$	42

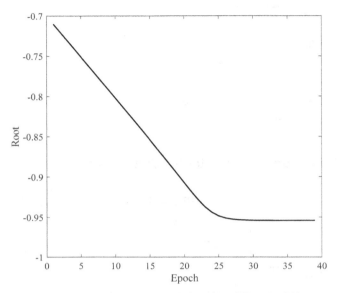

Fig. 3.11. First root (− 0.9541) of Eq. (3.13)

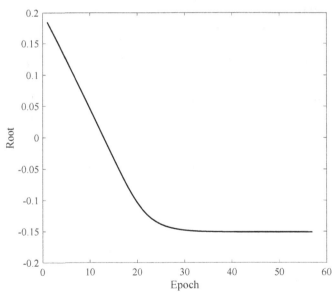

Fig. 3.12. Second root (− 0.1510) of Eq. (3.13).

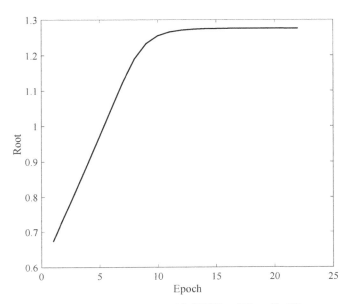

Fig. 3.13. Third root (1.2758) of Eq. (3.13)

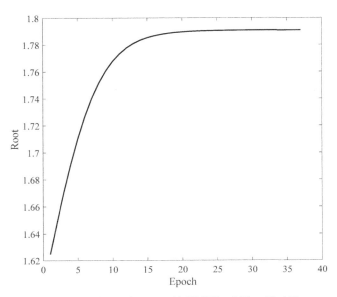

Fig. 3.14. Fourth root (1.7907) of Eq. (3.13).

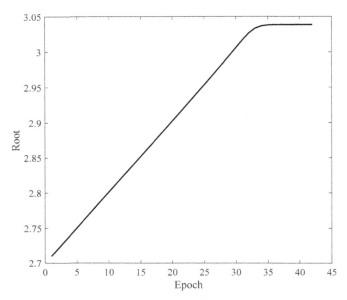

Fig. 3.15. Fifth root (3.0385) of Eq. (3.13)

Example 3.4: Let us consider a polynomial equation

$$8x^8 + 6x^7 - 5x^6 + 12x^5 - 8x^4 - 3x^3 + 4x^2 - 2x - 100 = 0 \qquad (3.14)$$

which has two real roots as -1.8260 and 1.3033.

Similar to the previous three examples, the ANN method is implemented to solve Eq. (3.14). Here, we have selected the initial weight as 0.1 along with the learning parameter 0.001 to compute the first root (-1.8260) of Eq. (3.14). Similarly, the initial weight is chosen as 0.6 with the same learning parameter to get another real root as 1.3033. The convergence plots of the roots have been depicted in Figs. 3.16 and 3.17.

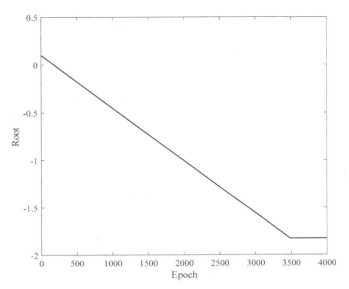

Fig. 3.16. First root (− 1.8260) of Eq. (3.14)

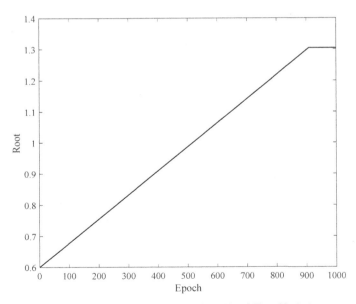

Fig. 3.17. Second root (1.3033) of Eq. (3.14).

Four examples of polynomial equations with different degrees (as above) have been solved using the proposed ANN procedure. As seen from the above examples, the ANN-based technique is helpful in solving polynomial equations.

These polynomial equations have various real-world applications. In this regard, an application problem for a bakery has been examined in the next section.

3.4 Bakery Problem

A bakery offers cakes for parties. The volume of a small cake is to be 351 in^3 and shape is of rectangular solid. Moreover, the bakery wants the length and height of the cake to be four inches and $1/3^{rd}$ of the width of the cake, respectively. The dimension of the cake pan is to be computed.

Volume of a rectangular solid is given by

$$V = lwh \qquad (3.15)$$

where l is the length, w is the width and h is the height.

As given earlier, the length and height of the cake are expressed as $l = w + 4$ and $h = 1/3w$, respectively.

Now, Eq. (3.15) can be rewritten as

$$V = (w+4)w((1/3)w)$$

$$\Rightarrow 351 = 1/3w^3 + 4/3w^2$$

$$\Rightarrow w^3 + 4w^2 - 1053 = 0 \qquad (3.16)$$

Thus, the bakery problem reduces to a polynomial equation. As such, the ANN model is trained with initial weight 0.4 to find the only real root as 9. Here, we have considered the learning parameter as 0.001. Figure 3.18 shows the convergence plot of the root.

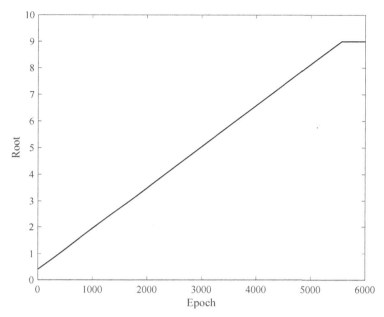

Fig. 3.18. Root of Eq. (3.16).

So, 9 is one of the solutions of Eq. (3.16). Therefore, length and height can be computed as

$l = w + 4 = 13$ and $h = 1/3w = 3$

Finally, the sheet cake pan has the dimensions 13 in by 9 in by 3 in.

3.5 Conclusion

In this chapter, an ANN-based procedure has been addressed to solve polynomial equations. Step-by-step procedure with the ANN model for handling polynomial equations has been discussed for clear understanding. Four example problems with an application problem for a bakery have been investigated. Finally, convergence tables and/or plots for the solutions of different example problems have also been included.

References

[1] B. Sendov, A. Andreev, and N. Kjurkchiev, (1994). Numerical solution of polynomial equations. *Handbook of Numerical Analysis*, *3*, 625–778.

[2] F. B. Hildebrand, (1987). *Introduction to Numerical Analysis*. Courier Corporation.

[3] W. Gautschi, (1997). *Numerical Analysis*. Springer Science & Business Media.

[4] C. F. Gerald, (2004). *Applied Numerical Analysis*. Pearson Education India.

[5] R. B. Bhat and S. Chakraverty, (2004). *Numerical Analysis in Engineering*. Alpha Science Int'l Ltd.

[6] K. E. Atkinson, (2008). *An Introduction to Numerical Analysis*. John wiley & sons.

[7] D. Kincaid, D. R. Kincaid, and E. W. Cheney, (2009). *Numerical analysis: Mathematics of scientific computing* (Vol. 2). American Mathematical Soc.

[8] J. Stoer and R. Bulirsch, (2013). *Introduction to Numerical Analysis* (Vol. 12). Springer Science & Business Media.

[9] S. D. Conte and C. De Boor, (2017). *Elementary numerical analysis: An algorithmic approach*. Society for Industrial and Applied Mathematics.

[10] V. Y. Pan, (1997). Solving a polynomial equation: Some history and recent progress. *SIAM Review*, *39*(2), 187–220.

[11] R. G. Kulkarni, (2006). Unified method for solving general polynomial equations of degree less than five. *Alabama Journal of Mathematics*, *30*(1), 1–18.

4

Transcendental Equations in Power Electronics Applications

This chapter presents an ANN-based method for solving transcendental equations. In this context, a multi-layer ANN model has been developed to handle transcendental equations. Different examples with an application problem for power electronics have been investigated here. Convergence tables and/or plots for the solutions of the different examples have also been included.

4.1 Introduction

An equation involving different transcendental functions is known as a transcendental equation. Transcendental equations have various applications in different fields viz. power electronics modeling, analytic geometry and automatics, etc. However, there exist various traditional numerical methods to handle transcendental equations, but these methods have certain limitations such as sign change, nonexistence of derivative, choosing the proper initial guess, etc. In this scenario, ANN may be a useful technique to solve those equations.

Different known numerical methods for solving transcendental equations can be found in [1–9]. Further, a novel method based on Cauchy's integral theorem has been proposed by Luck and Stevens [10] for finding the explicit solutions for transcendental equations. Li [11] presented a fast and stable algorithm based on Newton–Raphson method and the characteristics of the tangent function for solving transcendental equations. A genetic algorithm-based approach for solving transcendental equations has been proposed by Moazzam *et al.* [12]. Jeswal and Chakraverty [13] discussed an ANN-based technique for solving transcendental equations.

4.2 General Model of a Transcendental Equation

The general model of a transcendental equation may be defined as

$$a_1 e^x + a_2 \log x + \cdots + a_n \sin x = a_0 \tag{4.1}$$

where $a_1, a_2, \cdots, a_n$ are the different coefficients, $e^x, \log x, \sin x$ may be different transcendental functions and a_0 is the constant term.

An ANN architecture for solving Eq. (4.1) has been depicted in Fig. 4.1.

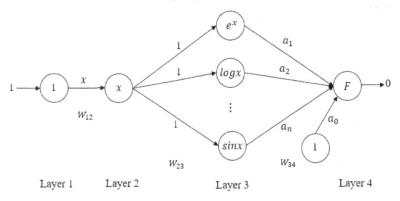

Fig. 4.1. ANN architecture for Eq. (4.1).

Generalized architecture for solving transcendental equation is shown in Fig. 4.1, which comprises of four layers, that is Layer 1 (input layer), Layers 2 and 3 (hidden layers) and Layer 4 (output layer). Input layer consists of one linear unit node with a constant input equal to unity. Further, first hidden layer (Layer 2) has one node for the linear term x and Layer 3 comprises a number of nodes depending upon the transcendental equation. Finally, output layer consists of summation units whose total input is the expression of the left-hand side of Eq. (4.1). It may be seen in Fig. 4.1 that weights from Layer 2 to Layer 3 are fixed, that is unity. Different coefficients of Eq. (4.1) are considered as the weights between Layers 3 and 4. There is only variable weight joining Layer 1 to 2, which is the solution of Eq. (4.1). There is also a bias node connecting to the output node and W_{ij} denotes the weights between the layers i and j. Further, the weights are written in matrix form as follows:

$$W_{12} = [W_{12}^{(1)}] = [x]$$

$$W_{23} = \begin{bmatrix} W_{23}^{(11)} \\ W_{23}^{(21)} \\ \vdots \\ W_{23}^{(n1)} \end{bmatrix} = \begin{bmatrix} 1 \\ 1 \\ \vdots \\ 1 \end{bmatrix}$$

$$W_{34} = \begin{bmatrix} W_{34}^{(11)} \\ W_{34}^{(21)} \\ \vdots \\ W_{34}^{(n1)} \end{bmatrix} = \begin{bmatrix} a_1 \\ a_2 \\ \vdots \\ a_n \end{bmatrix}$$

where, the subscripts 1, 2, 3, 4 denote the different layers of the ANN model.

4.3 Numerical Examples

In this section, six different examples of transcendental equations have been solved using the ANN procedure given in Section 3.2, Chapter 3. Convergence plots/tables for roots of the examples have also been demonstrated.

Example 4.1: Let us consider the transcendental equation

$$e^x - x - 2 = 0 \tag{4.2}$$

which has two real roots as 1.1462 and -1.8414.

Equation (4.2) is solved using the ANN procedure. ANN model for Eq. (4.2) has been constructed in Fig. 4.2.

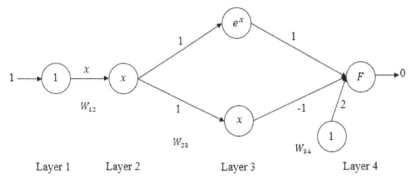

Fig. 4.2. ANN model for Eq. (4.2).

Initial weight (or guess) for finding the first root of Eq. (4.2) has been arbitrarily chosen as 0.1. Starting with the initial weight, the ANN procedure is applied to get the converged root as 1.1462. Similarly, -0.1 is taken as the initial weight for finding the second root, which is found to be -1.8414. The learning parameter for finding both the roots is taken as 0.9. Successive simulation results with respect to the different stopping criteria and number of epochs for the two roots have been included in Tables 4.1 and 4.2, respectively. Convergence plots of the roots have been depicted in Figs. 4.3 and 4.4.

Table 4.1. Convergence table for the first root of Eq. (4.2).

Root	Stopping Criteria	Epoch
0.1424	< 0.5	2
0.9160	< 0.1	21
1.0932	$< 10^{-2}$	29
1.1320	$< 10^{-3}$	35
1.1416	$< 10^{-4}$	40
1.1447	$< 10^{-5}$	45
1.1457	$< 10^{-6}$	50

1.1460	$< 10^{-7}$	55
1.1461	$< 10^{-8}$	60
1.1462	$< 10^{-9}$	65
1.1462	$< 10^{-10}$	70

Table 4.2. Convergence table for the second root of Eq. (4.2).

Root	Stopping Criteria	Epoch
-0.1383	< 0.5	2
-1.2742	< 0.1	33
-1.6866	$< 10^{-2}$	53
-1.7936	$< 10^{-3}$	69
-1.8269	$< 10^{-4}$	85
-1.8367	$< 10^{-5}$	100
-1.8399	$< 10^{-6}$	115
-1.8409	$< 10^{-7}$	131
-1.8414	$< 10^{-8}$	146
-1.8414	$< 10^{-9}$	162

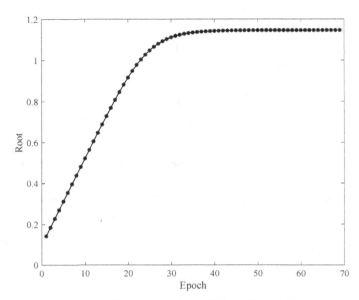

Fig. 4.3. First root (1.1462) of Eq. (4.2).

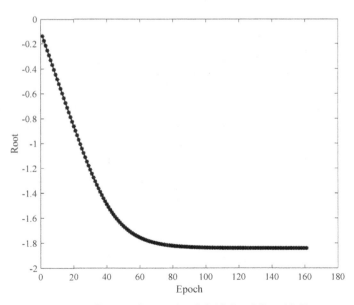

Fig. 4.4. Second root (− 1.8414) of Eq. (4.2).

Example 4.2: In the following example, a transcendental equation is considered

$$\cot x = e^x \tag{4.3}$$

Let us aim to find one positive and one negative real root for the above equation. From traditional methods, the positive and negative real roots may be obtained as 0.5314 and -1.7439, respectively.

An ANN architecture for Eq. (4.3) has been constructed in Fig. 4.5.

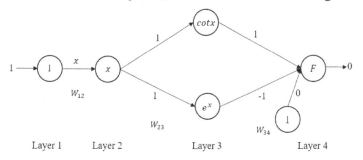

Fig. 4.5. ANN model for Eq. (4.3).

The ANN method is used to solve Eq. (4.3) by choosing initial weights as 0.1 and -0.1 for the positive and negative roots, respectively, with learning parameter 0.001. Successive simulation results for the two roots with respect to the different stopping criteria and number of epochs have been included in Tables 4.3 and 4.4. It may be seen from Tables 4.3 and 4.4 that initial weights converged to the desired roots viz. 0.5314 and $-$ 1.7439. Figures 4.6 and 4.7 demonstrate the convergence plots of the roots.

Table 4.3. Convergence table for the positive real root of Eq. (4.3).

Root	Stopping Criteria	Epoch
0.1426	<0.5	2
0.5109	<0.1	11
0.5266	$<10^{-2}$	12

0.5298	$<10^{-3}$	14
0.5307	$<10^{-4}$	15
0.5311	$<10^{-5}$	16
0.5313	$<10^{-6}$	18
0.5314	$<10^{-7}$	19
0.5314	$<10^{-8}$	20
0.5314	$<10^{-9}$	22

Table 4.4. Convergence table for the negative real root of Eq. (4.3).

Root	Stopping Criteria	Epoch
-0.1425	<0.5	2
-1.3934	<0.1	31
-1.6483	$<10^{-2}$	42
-1.7139	$<10^{-3}$	51
-1.7346	$<10^{-4}$	60
-1.7410	$<10^{-5}$	69
-1.7429	$<10^{-6}$	77
-1.7436	$<10^{-7}$	86
-1.7438	$<10^{-8}$	95
-1.7439	$<10^{-9}$	104
-1.7439	$<10^{-10}$	113

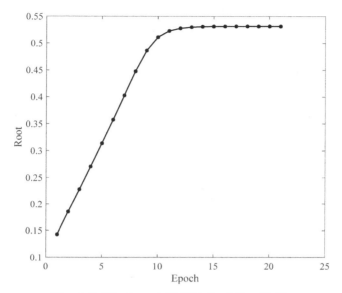

Fig. 4.6. First root (0.5314) of Eq. (4.3).

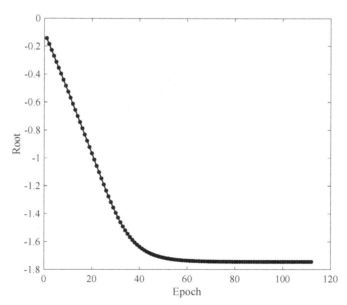

Fig. 4.7. Second root (− 1.7439) of Eq. (4.3).

Example 4.3: A transcendental equation is taken in this example

$$\sin x = 10(x - 1) \qquad (4.4)$$

which has a real root as 1.0886.

Here, we have considered the initial weight as 0.01 with the learning parameter 0.01 to compute the root as 1.0886. Simulation results along with the convergence plot of the root have been illustrated in Table 4.5 and Fig. 4.8, respectively.

Table 4.5. Convergence table for the root of Eq. (4.4).

Root	Stopping Criteria	Epoch
0.0478	< 0.5	2
1.0855	< 0.1	30
1.0882	$< 10^{-2}$	31
1.0882	$< 10^{-3}$	31
1.0885	$< 10^{-4}$	32
1.0885	$< 10^{-5}$	32
1.0886	$< 10^{-6}$	33
1.0886	$< 10^{-7}$	34
1.0886	$< 10^{-8}$	34

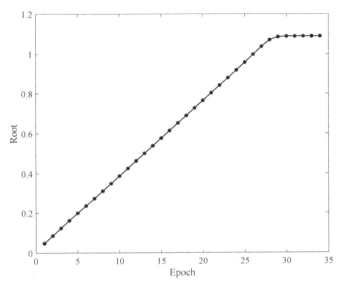

Fig. 4.8. Root (1.0886) of Eq. (4.4).

Example 4.4: Let us consider another transcendental equation

$$2x - \log_{10} x = 7 \tag{4.5}$$

which has a real root as 3.7893.

For solving Eq. (4.5), the ANN method is used by choosing initial weight as 0.2 with learning parameter 0.09. Here, the root is found as 3.7893. Simulation result of the root has been included in Table 4.6. Figure 4.9 shows the convergence plot of the root.

Table 4.6. Convergence table for the root of Eq. (4.5).

Root	Stopping Criteria	Epoch
0.2691	< 0.5	2
3.6080	< 0.1	50
3.7429	$< 10^{-2}$	54

3.7740	$<10^{-3}$	57
3.7842	$<10^{-4}$	60
3.7881	$<10^{-5}$	64
3.7889	$<10^{-6}$	67
3.7892	$<10^{-7}$	70
3.7892	$<10^{-8}$	73
3.7893	$<10^{-9}$	76
3.7893	$<10^{-10}$	79
3.7893	$<10^{-11}$	82
3.7893	$<10^{-12}$	85

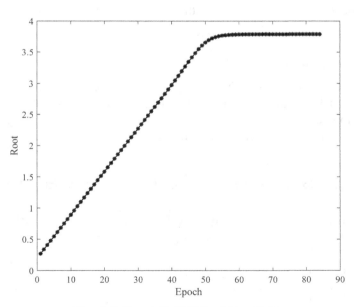

Fig. 4.9. Root (3.7893) of Eq. (4.5).

Example 4.5: Further, the transcendental equation is considered as

$$xe^x = \cos x \qquad (4.6)$$

Here, our target is to find the first three real roots of Eq. (4.6). Using the known traditional methods, the first three real roots may be found as 0.5178, -1.8640 and -4.6686.

Similar to the previous four examples, this transcendental equation has also been solved using the ANN procedure. Let us consider the initial weight and learning parameter as 0.01 and 0.1, respectively, to find the first root (0.5178) of Eq. (4.6). Similarly, -0.6 and -6 are chosen as initial weights with corresponding learning parameters 0.5 and 0.9, respectively, for computing the second (-1.8640) and third (-4.6686) roots. Tables 4.7 to 4.9 include the simulation results of the above roots for Eq. (4.6). Convergence plots of the roots have been depicted in Figs. 4.10 to 4.12.

Table 4.7. Convergence table for the first root of Eq. (4.6).

First root	Stopping Criteria	Epoch
0.0561	< 0.5	2
0.4175	< 0.1	9
0.5002	$< 10^{-2}$	12
0.5135	$< 10^{-3}$	14
0.5157	$< 10^{-4}$	15
0.5173	$< 10^{-5}$	17
0.5176	$< 10^{-6}$	19
0.5177	$< 10^{-7}$	20
0.5177	$< 10^{-8}$	22
0.5178	$< 10^{-9}$	23

0.5178	$< 10^{-10}$	25
0.5178	$< 10^{-11}$	26
0.5178	$< 10^{-12}$	28

Table 4.8. Convergence table for the second root of Eq. (4.6).

Second root	Stopping Criteria	Epoch
-0.6770	< 0.5	2
-1.5692	< 0.1	12
-1.7721	$< 10^{-2}$	16
-1.8382	$< 10^{-3}$	20
-1.8568	$< 10^{-4}$	24
-1.8613	$< 10^{-5}$	27
-1.8632	$< 10^{-6}$	31
-1.8637	$< 10^{-7}$	34
-1.8639	$< 10^{-8}$	38
-1.8640	$< 10^{-9}$	42
-1.8640	$< 10^{-10}$	45
-1.8640	$< 10^{-11}$	49

Table 4.9. Convergence table for the third root of Eq. (4.6).

Third root	Stopping Criteria	Epoch
-5.8925	<0.5	2
-5.0268	<0.1	11
-4.7652	$<10^{-2}$	17
-4.6995	$<10^{-3}$	22
-4.6785	$<10^{-4}$	27
-4.6718	$<10^{-5}$	32
-4.6696	$<10^{-6}$	37
-4.6689	$<10^{-7}$	42
-4.6687	$<10^{-8}$	47
-4.6686	$<10^{-9}$	52
-4.6686	$<10^{-10}$	57

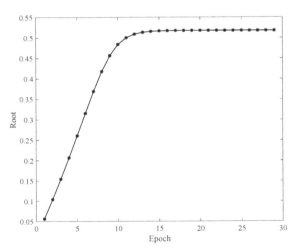

Fig. 4.10. First root (0.5178) of Eq. (4.6).

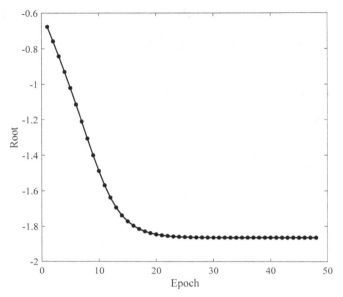

Fig. 4.11. Second root (-1.8640) of Eq. (4.6).

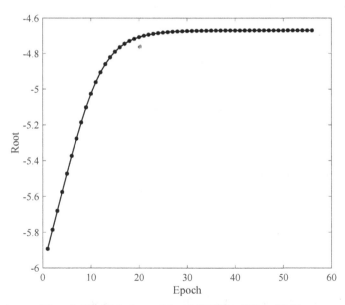

Fig. 4.12. Third root (-4.6686) of Eq. (4.6).

Example 4.6: The following example investigates the transcendental equation

$$x - 2\sin x = 0 \qquad\qquad (4.7)$$

Using traditional methods, one real root may be obtained as 1.8955.

The ANN method gives the desired solution 1.8955 starting with the initial guess value 1.1. The learning parameter is chosen as 0.9. Simulation result of the root has been given in Table 4.10 and corresponding plot is depicted in Fig. 4.13.

Table 4.10. Convergence table for the root of Eq. (4.7).

Root	Stopping Criteria	Epoch
1.1355	< 0.5	2
1.5720	< 0.1	15
1.8155	$< 10^{-2}$	27
1.8731	$< 10^{-3}$	36
1.8885	$< 10^{-4}$	44
1.8933	$< 10^{-5}$	52
1.8948	$< 10^{-6}$	60
1.8953	$< 10^{-7}$	68
1.8954	$< 10^{-8}$	75
1.8955	$< 10^{-9}$	83
1.8955	$< 10^{-10}$	90

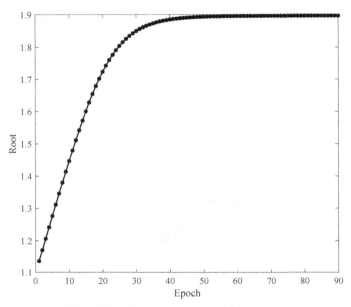

Fig. 4.13. Root (1.8955) of Eq. (4.7).

Six examples of transcendental equations have been solved using the ANN-based technique. It may be seen from the examples that, starting with random initial guesses, the ANN method converges to the desired solutions with ease.

4.4 Application Problem

An application problem of diode circuit analysis has been examined in this section. The main aim of diode circuit analysis is to find the quiescent operating point (Q-point) of the diode. Figure 4.14 shows a diode circuit.

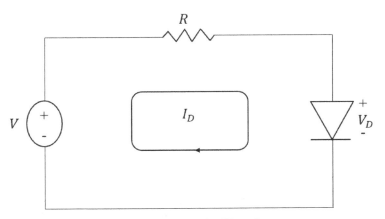

Fig. 4.14. Diode Circuit.

Diode equation is given by [14]

$$I_D = I_S\left(\exp\left(\frac{V_D}{V_T}\right) - 1\right) \tag{4.8}$$

where I_D : DC current

$\quad$ I_S : Reverse saturation current

$\quad$ V_D : Voltage

$\quad$ $V_T = kT/q$: Thermal voltage

Kirchhoff's Voltage Law along the loop is written as

$$V = I_D R + V_D \tag{4.9}$$

where V : source of the diode

$\quad$ R : load of the diode

Given $I_S = 10^{-13}$ A, $V_T = 25\,\mathrm{mV}$, $V = 10\,\mathrm{V}$, $R = 10\,\mathrm{k\Omega}$, let us find the Q-point of the diode.

From the given data, Eqs. (4.8) and (4.9) can be computed as

$$\begin{cases} I_D = 10^{-13}\left(\exp\left(\dfrac{V_D}{25\times10^{-3}}\right)-1\right) = 10^{-13}\left(\exp\left(40V_D\right)-1\right) \\ 10 = I_D 10^4 + V_D \end{cases} \quad (4.10)$$

From Eq. (4.10), we have

$$10 - V_D = 10^4 10^{-13}\left(\exp\left(40V_D\right)-1\right)$$

$$\Rightarrow 10^{-9}\exp\left(40V_D\right) + V_D - (10^{-9}+10) = 0 \quad (4.11)$$

Equation (4.11) is a transcendental equation which can be solved using the ANN procedure. The converged solution is found as 0.5742 in this case. Successive simulation result along with the convergence plot of root for Eq. (4.11) has been shown in Table 4.11 and Fig. 4.15, respectively.

Table 4.11. Convergence table for the root of Eq. (4.11).

Root	Stopping Criteria	Epoch
0.6008	< 0.5	52
0.5752	< 0.1	148
0.5745	$< 10^{-2}$	156
0.5743	$< 10^{-3}$	164
0.5742	$< 10^{-4}$	171
0.5742	$< 10^{-5}$	179
0.5742	$< 10^{-6}$	186

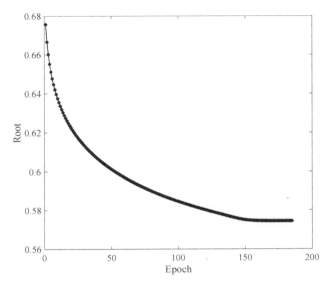

Fig. 4.15. Root (0.5742) of the Eq. (4.11).

The result obtained from the ANN method may be verified by putting the root in Eq. (4.11).

4.5 Conclusion

A novel technique based on the concept of ANN has been included in this chapter for solving transcendental equations. In this regard, a four-layer ANN architecture has been developed to handle the titled problem. Different examples with an application problem for power electronics have been investigated to show the efficiency of the ANN method. The convergence plots and/or tables for the solutions of different examples have also been illustrated.

References

[1] F. B. Hildebrand, (1987). *Introduction to Numerical Analysis.* Courier Corporation.

[2] W. Gautschi, (1997). *Numerical Analysis.* Springer Science & Business Media.

[3] A. Neumaier, (2001). *Introduction to Numerical Analysis.* Cambridge University Press.

[4] T. Sauer, (2006). *Numerical Analysis.* Pearson Addison Wesley.

[5] U. M. Ascher and C. Greif, (2011). *A First Course on Numerical Methods* (Vol. 7). Siam.

[6] S. S. Sastry, (2012). *Introductory Methods of Numerical Analysis.* PHI Learning Pvt. Ltd.

[7] B. Ayyub and R. H. McCuen, (2015). *Numerical Analysis for Engineers: Methods and Applications.* CRC Press.

[8] A. C. Faul, (2016). *A Concise Introduction to Numerical Analysis.* CRC Press.

[9] V. L. Zaguskin, (2014). *Handbook of numerical methods for the solution of algebraic and transcendental equations.* Elsevier.

[10] R. Luck and J. W. Stevens, (2002). Explicit solutions for transcendental equations. *SIAM Review, 44*(2), 227–233.

[11] Z. Li, (2012). Numerical evaluations of transcendental equations for transient experiments. *International Journal of Hydrogen Energy, 37*(9), 8118–8122.

[12] M. G. Moazzam, A. Chakraborty, and M. A. A. Bhuiyan, (2012). A robust method for solving transcendental equations. *International Journal of Computer Science Issues (IJCSI), 9*(6), 413.

[13] S. K. Jeswal and S. Chakraverty, (2018). Solving transcendental equation using artificial neural network. *Applied Soft Computing, 73,* 562–571.

[14] M. Tooley, (2007). *Electronic Circuits-Fundamentals & Applications.* Routledge.

5

Diophantine Equations in Pole Placement

In this chapter, an ANN method has been introduced to find the numerical solutions of various Diophantine equations. A multi-layer ANN model has been constructed in this regard. Different examples have been solved to show the efficacy of the method. Further, an application of Diophantine equation in pole placement has also been investigated.

5.1 Introduction

Diophantine equations are not only an important concept but also the basis of number theory. As we know, Diophantine equation is a type of polynomial equation having fewer equations as compared to the number of variables. Only the integer solutions have been studied in case of Diophantine equations. Here, a novel approach based on the concept of ANN has been addressed to solve Diophantine equations.

Different methods have been proposed for handling Diophantine equations. In this context, Clausen and Fortenbacher [1] found all the nonnegative integer solutions of linear Diophantine equations. Polynomial solutions of Diophantine equations have been computed by Yamada and Funahashi [2]. Abraham *et al.* [3] presented an ant colony optimization-based technique to find the numerical solutions of Diophantine equations. A particle swarm optimization algorithm has been proposed by Pérez *et al.* [4] for finding the numerical solutions of exponential and nonlinear Diophantine systems of equations. Amaya *et al.* [5] solved a linear system of Diophantine equations numerically using a discrete particle swarm optimization technique. Recently, Jeswal and Chakraverty [6] discussed an ANN procedure for finding the numerical solutions of Diophantine equations. Further, basics related to Diophantine equations can be found in some standard books [7–14].

5.2 General Model of a Diophantine Equation

A general model of a nonlinear Diophantine equation [3, 7] may be written as

$$a_1 x_1^k + a_2 x_2^k + \cdots + a_n x_n^k = d \tag{5.1}$$

where $a_1, a_2, \cdots, a_n$ are the different coefficients, $x_1, x_2, \cdots, x_n$ are the unknown variables, d is an integer and k, n are positive integers. Equation (5.1) has a solution if and only if d divides $gcd(a_1, a_2, \cdots, a_n)$.

There may be different cases depending upon the number of variables:

(1) Two parameter case: $a_1 x_1^k + a_2 x_2^k = d$
(2) Three parameter case: $a_1 x_1^k + a_2 x_2^k + a_3 x_3^k = d$
(3) Four parameter case: $a_1 x_1^k + a_2 x_2^k + a_3 x_3^k + a_4 x_4^k = d$

and so on.

5.2.1 ANN Procedure for Solving Diophantine Equation

The ANN model for handling Eq. (5.1) has been illustrated in Fig. 5.1.

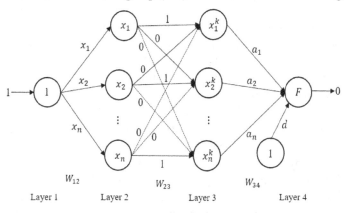

Fig. 5.1. Multi-layer ANN architecture.

General model of the Diophantine equation has been shown in Fig. 5.1. This model consists of four layers, that is Layer 1 (input layer), Layers 2 and 3 (hidden layers) and Layer 4 (output layer). The input layer consists of one linear unit node with a constant input equal to unity. Further, the first hidden layer (Layer 2) has n nodes for the linear terms $x_1, x_2, \cdots, x_n$ and the next hidden layer comprises a number of nodes depending upon the Diophantine equation. Finally, the output layer consists of summation units whose total input is the expression of the left-hand side of the Diophantine equation. It has been clearly shown in Fig. 5.1 that the weights from Layer 2 to Layer 3 are fixed depending upon the Diophantine equation. Different coefficients of the Diophantine equation are taken as the weights between Layer 3 and Layer 4. There are only variable weights joining Layer 1 to Layer 2, which is nothing but the solution of the given Diophantine equation. There is also a bias node connecting to the output node and W_{ij} denotes the weights between the layers i and j.

Various weight matrices between the layers are given as follows;

$$
W_{12} = \begin{bmatrix} W_{12}^{(1)} \\ W_{12}^{(2)} \\ \vdots \\ W_{12}^{(n)} \end{bmatrix} = \begin{bmatrix} x_1 \\ x_2 \\ \vdots \\ x_n \end{bmatrix}
$$

$$
W_{23} = \begin{bmatrix} W_{23}^{(11)} & W_{23}^{(12)} & \cdots & W_{23}^{(1n)} \\ W_{23}^{(21)} & W_{23}^{(22)} & \cdots & W_{23}^{(2n)} \\ \vdots & \vdots & \ddots & \vdots \\ W_{23}^{(n1)} & W_{23}^{(n2)} & \cdots & W_{23}^{(nn)} \end{bmatrix} = \begin{bmatrix} 1 & 0 & \cdots & 0 \\ 0 & 1 & \cdots & 0 \\ \vdots & \vdots & \ddots & \vdots \\ 0 & 0 & \cdots & 1 \end{bmatrix}
$$

$$
W_{34} = \begin{bmatrix} W_{34}^{(1)} \\ W_{34}^{(2)} \\ \vdots \\ W_{34}^{(n)} \end{bmatrix} = \begin{bmatrix} a_1 \\ a_2 \\ \vdots \\ a_n \end{bmatrix}
$$

where the subscripts 1, 2, 3, 4· denote the different layers of the ANN architecture.

The input–output relationship of the network architecture of the neurons is given by $u_k = f(U_k)$ ($k = 2,3,4$), where U is the input to the neuron, f

is its activation function and u is the produced output. The inputs with vector notations of different layers are written as follows:

$$U_2 = [U_2^{(1)} \quad U_2^{(2)} \quad \cdots \quad U_2^{(n)}] = [x_1 \quad x_2 \quad \cdots \quad x_n]$$

$$U_3 = [U_3^{(1)} \quad U_3^{(2)} \quad \cdots \quad U_3^{(n)}] = [x_1 \quad x_2 \quad \cdots \quad x_n]$$

$$U_4 = [U_4^{(1)}] = [F(x)]$$

We may use the activation functions for Layer 2 (Identity function), Layer 3 (Polynomial function) and Layer 4 (Tangent hyperbolic function) as follows:

$$f_2 = [f_2^{(1)}(U) \quad f_2^{(2)}(U) \quad \cdots \quad f_2^{(n)}(U)]$$

$$f_3 = [f_3^{(1)}(U) \quad f_3^{(2)}(U) \quad \cdots \quad f_3^{(n)}(U)]$$

$$f_4 = [f_4^{(1)}(U)] = [\tanh(U)]$$

corresponding outputs can be computed thus:

$$u_2 = [u_2^{(1)} \quad u_2^{(2)} \quad \cdots \quad u_2^{(n)}] = [x_1 \quad x_2 \quad \cdots \quad x_n]$$

$$u_3 = [u_3^{(1)} \quad u_3^{(2)} \quad \cdots \quad u_3^{(n)}] = [x_1^k \quad x_2^k \quad \cdots \quad x_n^k]$$

$$u_4 = [u_4^{(1)}] = [\tanh[F(x)]]$$

The well-known backpropagation algorithm is applied to solve the titled problem. As such, the forward and backward pass with weight update formula has been discussed further.

Forward Pass:

Using the backpropagation algorithm, the network input to the jth hidden neuron of any hidden layer is given by

$$net_j = \sum_{i=1}^{n} W_{ij} x_i + b_j$$

where W_{ij} is the weight from the input unit to the hidden unit, x_i is the input vector and b_j is the bias. Output of jth hidden neuron can be computed as

$$y_j = f(net_j)$$

where f is the activation function.

This concept may be used for the network and notations discussed in the previous section, which can be expressed as follows:

The input to the neurons of Layer 2 is written as

$$U_2^{(i)} = W_{12}^{(i)}, \text{ where } i = 1, 2, \cdots, n$$

and the corresponding output is given by

$$u_2^{(i)} = f_2^{(i)}(U_2^{(i)}) = x_i, \; i = 1, 2, \cdots, n$$

Layer 3 consists of n units corresponding to the values $i = 1, 2, \cdots, n$. The inputs to the n units are given as

$$U_3^{(i)} = W_{23}^{(ij)} u_2^{(i)}, \tag{5.2}$$

The outputs of Layer 3 can be found as

$$u_3^{(i)} = f_3^{(i)}(U_3^{(i)}) = x_i^k, \; i = 1, 2, \cdots, n$$

The input to the linear neurons of Layer 4 is calculated as

$$U_4^{(1)} = \sum_{i=1}^{n} W_{34}^{(i1)} u_3^{(i)} - d = F(x) \tag{5.3}$$

and the corresponding output is calculated as

$$U_4^{(1)} \equiv o = \tanh(U_4^{(1)}) = \tanh[F(x)] \tag{5.4}$$

Backward Pass:

The different parameters in case of backward pass for Layers 2, 3 and 4 are defined as

$$\gamma_2 = [\gamma_2^{(1)} \quad \gamma_2^{(2)} \quad \cdots \quad \gamma_2^{(n)}]$$

$$\gamma_3 = [\gamma_3^{(1)} \quad \gamma_3^{(2)} \quad \cdots \quad \gamma_3^{(n)}]$$

$$\gamma_4 = [\gamma_4^{(1)}]$$

Starting with the output layer and the ANN, output is of the form

$$o = \tanh[F(x)]$$

and the corresponding desired output is chosen as $h = 0$ while the activation function for Layer 4 is chosen to be a hyperbolic tangent function whose derivative is

$$\tanh'(x) = 1 - \tanh^2(x)$$

Then the element of γ_4 is estimated as

$$\gamma_4^{(1)} = (h - o)\tanh'(U_4^{(1)}) = -\tanh[F(x)](1 - \tanh^2[F(x)])$$

Further using the γ_4 value, the γ values of Layer 3 have been calculated as

$$\gamma_3^{(i)} = (W_{34}^{(i1)}\gamma_4^{(1)}) \cdot (f_3^{(i)'}(U_3^{(i)})) \text{, where } i = 1, 2, \cdots, n \tag{5.5}$$

and the different derivatives involved in Eq. (5.5) can be computed as

$$f_3^{(1)'}(U_3^{(1)}) = kx_1^{k-1}, \; f_3^{(2)'}(U_3^{(2)}) = kx_2^{k-1}, \cdots, \; f_3^{(n)'}(U_3^{(n)}) = kx_n^{k-1}.$$

Further, Eq. (5.5) is rewritten as

$$\gamma_3^{(i)} = (W_{34}^{(i1)}\gamma_4^{(1)})(kx_j^{k-1}) = [-f(F)(1 - f^2(F))](kx_j^{k-1}), \; j = 1, 2, \cdots, n$$

Finally, the γ value of Layer 2 is estimated using the γ_3 values computed in Eq. (5.5).

$$\gamma_2^{(i)} = \left(\sum_{j=1}^{n} W_{23}^{(ij)}\gamma_3^{(j)} \right) \cdot (f_2^{(i)'}(U_2^{(i)})), i = 1, 2, \cdots, n \tag{5.6}$$

where the derivative involved in Eq. (5.6) is equal to $f_2^{(i)'}(U_2^{(i)}) = 1$. As such, Eq. (5.6) is rewritten in the following form:

$$\gamma_2^{(i)} = \left(\sum_{j=1}^{n} W_{23}^{(ij)} \gamma_3^{(j)} \right) = \gamma_4^{(1)} \frac{\partial F(x)}{\partial x_i} , \quad i = 1, 2, \cdots, n$$

Updating weights of the network architecture:

The weight updating equation is written as

$$W_{12}^{(i)} = W_{12}^{(i)} + \eta \gamma_2^{(i)} = W_{12}^{(i)} + \eta \gamma_4^{(1)} \frac{\partial F(x)}{\partial W_{12}^{(i)}}, i = 1, 2, \cdots, n \qquad (5.7)$$

where η is the learning parameter.

The mean square error is calculated as

$$E = \frac{1}{2}(h-o)^2 = \frac{1}{2} f^2 [F(x)] \qquad (5.8)$$

Differentiating Eq. (3.8) with respect to $W_{12}^{(i)}$, we have

$$\frac{\partial E}{\partial W_{12}^{(i)}} = -f(F(x))(1 - f^2(F(x))) \frac{\partial F(x)}{\partial W_{12}^{(i)}} = -\gamma_4^{(1)} \frac{\partial F(x)}{\partial W_{12}^{(i)}} \qquad (5.9)$$

Finally, the weight update equation is

$$W_{12}^{(i)} = W_{12}^{(i)} - \eta \frac{\partial E}{\partial W_{12}^{(i)}}, \quad i = 1, 2, \cdots, n \qquad (5.10)$$

5.3 Numerical Examples

Different example problems of Diophantine equations have been solved in this section. These examples have been divided into two cases. In the first case, the power (k) of Eq. (5.1) is fixed and the number of variables (n) will vary. The first three examples viz. examples 5.1, 5.2 and 5.3 have been solved in this context.

On the other hand, in examples 5.4, 5.5 and 5.6 the number of variables (n) is fixed and power (k) varies.

Example 5.1: Let us consider a Diophantine equation [3]

$$x_1^2 + x_2^2 + x_3^2 + x_4^2 + x_5^2 = 325 \qquad (5.11)$$

which has a solution as (2,5,6,8,14).

The ANN architecture for solving Eq. (5.11) can be visualized as Fig. 5.2.

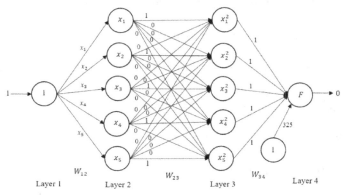

Fig. 5.2. ANN model for Eq. (5.11).

Although the detailed technique for solving Diophantine equations has been presented in Section 5.2.1, a few steps of the procedure have been discussed again for clear understanding. From Fig. 5.2, it is seen that the ANN model consists of four layers, that is Layer 1 (input layer), Layers 2 and 3 (hidden layers) and Layer 4 (output layer). There is only variable weight joining Layer 1 to Layer 2, which is nothing but the solution of Eq. (5.11).

Various weight matrices between the layers are as follows:

$$W_{12} = \begin{bmatrix} W_{12}^{(1)} \\ W_{12}^{(2)} \\ W_{12}^{(3)} \\ W_{12}^{(4)} \\ W_{12}^{(5)} \end{bmatrix} = \begin{bmatrix} x_1 \\ x_2 \\ x_3 \\ x_4 \\ x_5 \end{bmatrix}$$

$$W_{23} = \begin{bmatrix} W_{23}^{(11)} & W_{23}^{(11)} & W_{23}^{(11)} & W_{23}^{(11)} & W_{23}^{(11)} \\ W_{23}^{(21)} & W_{23}^{(21)} & W_{23}^{(21)} & W_{23}^{(21)} & W_{23}^{(21)} \\ W_{23}^{(31)} & W_{23}^{(31)} & W_{23}^{(31)} & W_{23}^{(31)} & W_{23}^{(31)} \\ W_{23}^{(31)} & W_{23}^{(31)} & W_{23}^{(31)} & W_{23}^{(31)} & W_{23}^{(31)} \\ W_{23}^{(31)} & W_{23}^{(31)} & W_{23}^{(31)} & W_{23}^{(31)} & W_{23}^{(31)} \end{bmatrix} = \begin{bmatrix} 1 & 0 & 0 & 0 & 0 \\ 0 & 1 & 0 & 0 & 0 \\ 0 & 0 & 1 & 0 & 0 \\ 0 & 0 & 0 & 1 & 0 \\ 0 & 0 & 0 & 0 & 1 \end{bmatrix}$$

$$W_{34} = \begin{bmatrix} W_{34}^{(1)} \\ W_{34}^{(2)} \\ W_{34}^{(3)} \\ W_{34}^{(4)} \\ W_{34}^{(5)} \end{bmatrix} = \begin{bmatrix} 1 \\ 1 \\ 1 \\ 1 \\ 1 \end{bmatrix}$$

where the subscripts 1, 2, 3, 4 denote the different layers of the ANN model.

As such, the ANN procedure is applied to solve Eq. (5.11). Let us consider the initial weights and learning parameter as (0.02, 0.05, 0.06, 0.08, 0.14) and 0.1, respectively, to obtain the desired solution as (2, 5, 6, 8, 14). Figure 5.3 shows the convergence plot of the solution.

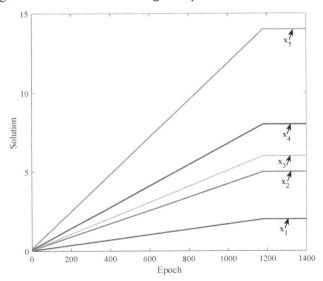

Fig. 5.3. Convergence plot for the solution of Eq. (5.11).

It may be seen from Fig. 5.3 that the solution started converging after nearly 1200 epochs and gives the desired solution.

Example 5.2: Further, another Diophantine equation is considered as follows:

$$2x_1^2 + 2x_2^2 + 4x_3^2 + 6x_4^2 + 8x_5^2 = 2154 \qquad (5.12)$$

which has a solution as (2, 5, 6, 8, 14).

The ANN technique has been implemented for solving Eq. (5.12). Here, the initial weights and learning parameter are considered as (0.3633, 0.91, 0.6, 0.551, 0.736) and 0.0001, respectively. The numerical solution for Eq. (5.12) can be found as (2, 5.0096, 6.0060, 7.9978, 13.9988) whose convergence plot has been depicted in Fig. 5.4.

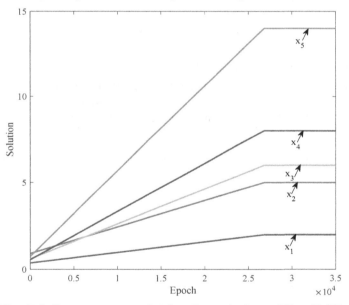

Fig. 5.4. Convergence plot for the solution of Eq. (5.12).

Example 5.3: The following Diophantine equation is examined next

$$x_1^2 + x_2^2 + \cdots + x_{11}^2 = 4466 \qquad (5.13)$$

which has a solution as (4, 6, 8, 10, 14, 18, 20, 23, 26, 30, 35).

The ANN model is trained with arbitrary weights along with learning parameter 0.01 to get the desired solution. Figure 5.5 shows the convergence plot of the solution for Eq. (5.13).

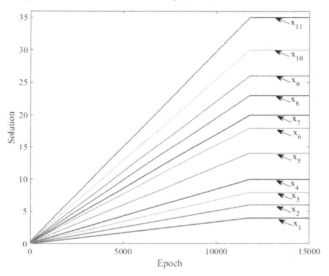

Fig. 5.5. Convergence plot for the solution of Eq. (5.13).

In the following three examples, the number of variables (n) is fixed and the power (k) of Eq. (5.1) varies.

Example 5.4: Solve the following Diophantine equation [3]

$$x_1^7 + x_2^7 = 4799353 \tag{5.14}$$

which has a solution as (4, 9).

The ANN architecture for Eq. (5.14) has been constructed as Fig. 5.6.

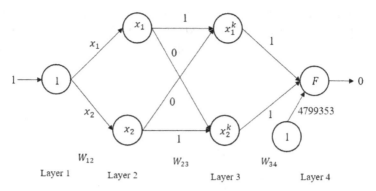

Fig. 5.6. ANN model for Eq. (5.14).

Equation (5.14) is solved using the ANN method. In this case, the initial weights and learning parameter are chosen as (0.5, 0.5786) and 0.0001, respectively. The numerical solution has been found as (4.0070, 8.9999) whose convergence plot has been illustrated in Fig. 5.7.

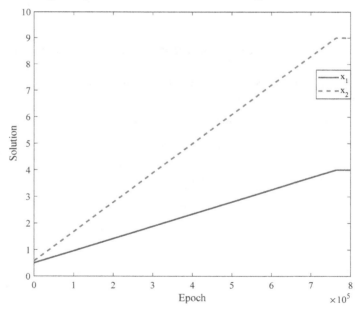

Fig. 5.7. Convergence plot for the solution of Eq. (5.14).

Example 5.5: Another Diophantine equation is considered as follows:

$$x_1^{12} + x_2^{12} = 244144721 \tag{5.15}$$

which has a solution as (2, 5).

The ANN procedure is applied to solve Eq. (5.15) by starting with the initial weights (0.5509, 0.6) and learning parameter 0.009. The numerical solution has been obtained as (2.0011, 5.0000). The convergence plot of the solution has been demonstrated in Fig. 5.8.

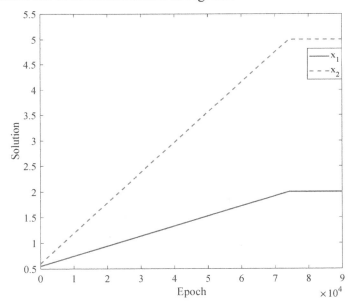

Fig. 5.8. Convergence plot for the solution of Eq. (5.15).

Example 5.6: Let us now consider a Diophantine equation

$$x_1^{15} + x_2^{15} = 1088090731 \tag{5.16}$$

which has a solution as (3, 4).

Similar to the previous examples, Eq. (5.16) is also solved using the ANN method. Initial weights and learning parameter are randomly chosen as (0.4883, 0.5) and 0.1, respectively. The final solution can be computed as (3.0008, 4.0000) and convergence plot for the same has been shown in Fig. 5.9.

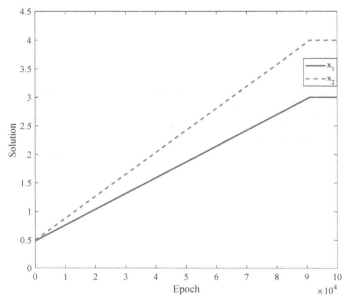

Fig. 5.9. Convergence plot for the solution of Eq. (5.16).

Six different Diophantine equations as above have been solved using the ANN procedure. It has been seen from these examples that the ANN method is effective in solving Diophantine equations. An application problem of pole placement has been investigated in the next section.

5.4 Application Problem

Let us consider an n-order plant $P(s)$ is $P(s) = \dfrac{a(s)}{b(s)}$, where

$a(s) = \sum_{i=0}^{n} p_i s^i$ and $b(s) = \sum_{i=n+1}^{2n} p_i s^{i-n-1}$ are polynomials with coefficients

p_i for $i = 1, 2, \cdots, 2n$. The m-order controller is $C(s) = \dfrac{A(s)}{B(s)}$, where

$A(s)$ and $B(s)$ are polynomials of degree $m < n$. Here, the main task is to design the controller $C(s)$ of order m.

The closed-loop system has a transfer function $T(s)$ given by [15]

$$T(s) = \frac{C(s)P(s)}{1 + C(s)P(s)} = \frac{B(s)b(s)}{A(s)a(s) + B(s)b(s)} \qquad (5.17)$$

Further, the pole placement problem may be considered as pole assignment of $T(s)$ by solving the polynomial equation

$$T'(s) = A(s)a(s) + B(s)b(s) \qquad (5.18)$$

where $T'(s) = \sum_{i=0}^{n+m} t_i s^i$ is the characteristic polynomial. Equation (5.18) is a Diophantine equation which can further be formulated as

$$\sum_{i=0}^{n+m} t_i s^i = \sum_{i=n+1}^{2n} p_i s^{i-n-1} \sum_{i=m+1}^{2m} c_i s^{i-m-1} + \sum_{i=0}^{n} p_i s^i \sum_{i=0}^{m} c_i s^i \qquad (5.19)$$

Again, Eq. (5.19) leads to a linear system of equations in terms of the unknown coefficients of $A(s)$ and $B(s)$ polynomials.

Let us consider a second-order plant system [16] $P(s) = \dfrac{s + p_0}{s^2 - 2.2s + p_3}$,

where $p_i = 1$ for $i = 0,3$ The associated closed-loop characteristic polynomial has been considered as $T'(s) = s^3 + 12s^2 + 21s + 15$.

Here, the linear control is assumed as

$$C(s) = \frac{B_0 + B_1 s}{A_0 + A_1 s} \qquad (5.20)$$

where the unknown coefficient B_i and A_i ($i = 0,1$) are to be determined.

The Diophantine equation for the system can be found as

$$(s^2 - 2.2s + p_3)(A_0 + A_1 s) + (s + p_0)(B_0 + B_1 s) = s^3 + 12s^2 + 21s + 15 \qquad (5.21)$$

Again, Eq. (5.21) transforms into a polynomial equation as

$$A_1 s^3 + (B_1 + A_0 - 2.2A_1)s^2 + (B_0 + B_1 + A_1 - 2.2A_0)s + (B_0 + A_0) = s^3 + 12s^2 + 21s + 15 \qquad (5.22)$$

Equation (5.22) is reduced to a linear system by comparing both sides of the equation with the power of s as

$$s^3 : A_1 = 1$$
$$s^2 : B_1 + A_0 - 2.2 A_1 = 12$$
$$s^1 : B_0 + B_1 + A_1 - 2.2 A_0 = 21$$
$$s^0 : B_0 + A_0 = 15$$

(5.23)

The above system can be written in the Sylvester matrix as

$$
\begin{bmatrix}
1 & 0 & 0 & 0 \\
-2.2 & 1 & 1 & 0 \\
1 & -2.2 & 1 & 1 \\
0 & 1 & 0 & 1
\end{bmatrix}
\begin{bmatrix}
A_1 \\
A_0 \\
B_1 \\
B_0
\end{bmatrix}
=
\begin{bmatrix}
1 \\
12 \\
21 \\
15
\end{bmatrix}
$$

(5.24)

Solving the system (5.24), different values are obtained as follows:

$$A_1 = 1, \quad A_0 = 2.1905, \quad B_1 = 12.0095, \quad B_0 = 12.8095$$

The final control can be found as

$$C(s) = \frac{12.8095 + 12.0095s}{2.1905 + s}$$

5.5 Conclusion

In this chapter, numerical solutions of various Diophantine equations have been found using the the ANN procedure. A multi-layer ANN architecture has been constructed for handling the Diophantine equations. The efficiency of the presented method has been verified by solving different examples. Further, convergence plots for the solutions of these examples have also been depicted. Finally, an application problem of pole placement has been investigated.

References

[1] M. Clausen and A. Fortenbacher, (1989). Efficient solution of linear diophantine equations. *Journal of Symbolic Computation*, 8(1–2), 201–216.

[2] M. Yamada and Y. Funahashi, (1994). A simple algorithm for solutions of diophantine equation. *Transactions of the Society of Instrument and Control Engineers*, *30*(3), 261–266.

[3] S. Abraham, S. Sanyal, and M. Sanglikar, (2013). Finding numerical solutions of diophantine equations using ant colony optimization. *Applied Mathematics and Computation*, *219*(24), 11376–11387.

[4] O. Pérez, I. Amaya, and R. Correa, (2013). Numerical solution of certain exponential and non-linear Diophantine systems of equations by using a discrete particle swarm optimization algorithm. *Applied Mathematics and Computation*, 225, 737–746.

[5] I. Amaya, L. Gómez, and R. Correa, (2014). Discrete particle swarm optimization in the numerical solution of a system of linear diophantine equations. *Dyna*, *81*(185), 139–144.

[6] S. K. Jeswal and S. Chakraverty, (2020). Connectionist based models for solving Diophantine equation. *Journal of Interdisciplinary Mathematics*, 1–17.

[7] D. M. Burton, (2006). Elementary number theory. Tata McGraw-Hill Education.

[8] L. K. Hua, (2012). *Introduction to Number Theory*. Springer Science & Business Media.

[9] T. M. Apostol, (2013). *Introduction to Analytic Number Theory*. Springer Science & Business Media.

[10] A. Weil, (2013). *Basic number theory* (Vol. 144). Springer Science & Business Media.

[11] K. H. Rosen, (2014). *Elementary number theory*. Pearson Education.

[12] H. Iwaniec and E. Kowalski, (2004). *Analytic number theory* (Vol. 53). American Mathematical Soc.

[13] H. Cohen, (2008). *Number theory: Volume II: Analytic and modern tools* (Vol. 240). Springer Science & Business Media.

[14] N. Koblitz, (1994). *A course in number theory and cryptography* (Vol. 114). Springer Science & Business Media.

[15] C. T. Chen, (1998). *Linear system theory and design*. Oxford University Press, Inc.

[16] A. D. Lordelo, E. A. Juzzo, and P. A. Ferreira, (2006). Analysis and design of robust controllers using the interval diophantine equation. *Reliable Computing, 12*(5), 371–388.

6

Systems of Linear Equations with Application in Static Structural Problems

An ANN-based technique for solving linear system of equations (LSEs) has been discussed in this chapter. A single-layer ANN model with a detailed procedure has been presented. Different examples of LSEs with an application of static structural problem have been solved. Moreover, an example has also been solved to show the efficiency of the ANN method over the known traditional method.

6.1 Introduction

Linear systems of equations (LSEs) have many applications in the field of mathematics and engineering. There are various methods known to solve LSEs such as Gauss elimination, Gauss Jordan, Cholesky, Jacobi, Gauss–Seidel and SOR method, etc. However, these methods may fail sometimes to handle LSEs, when the system is not diagonally dominant, positive definite, etc. As such, ANN may be an advantageous or alternate method to handle LSEs in these scenarios.

Different ANN methods have been proposed by various researchers to solve LSEs. In this regard, a neuron-like model has been discussed by Cichocki and Unbehauen [1] for high-speed computations of LSEs. Wang [2] introduced an electronic neural network for solving LSEs. An ANN-based parallel model has been presented by DeCarvalho and Barbosa [3] for handling LSEs. Wang and Li [4] used a recurrent neural network for solving LSEs. An ANN technique for solving ill-conditioned LSEs has been proposed by Li and Shang [5]. An ANN-based circuit has been constructed to solve LSEs by Rahman and Ansari [6]. Mall *et al.* [7] proposed ANN-based approaches for solving differential and integral equations. Further, different numerical methods for solving LSEs can be found in [8–11].

Various problems of engineering and science may transform to LSEs in particular static problems of structures in general transforms to LSEs. As such, the quadrature element method (QEM) has been introduced by Striz *et al.* [12] for static analysis of truss and frame structures. Differential quadrature element method (DQEM) has been presented by Wang and Gu [13] to analyze frame structures. Further, Wang *et al.* [14] extended the DQEM to investigate rectangular plate problems. A face-based smoothed radial point interpolation technique has been proposed by Feng *et al.* [15] for static analysis of structures. Catenary equation-based approach has been presented for the static analysis of three-dimensional cable structures by Such *et al.* [16]. Viola *et al.* [17] used the generalized differential finite element method and cell method for static analysis of composite plane state structures. Franciosi and Tomasiello [18] addressed a modified QEM to perform static analysis of structures. An antiprism tensegrity structure has been investigated by Crane *et al.* [19]. Static analysis of functionally graded carbon nanotube-reinforced plate and shell structures have been examined by Zghal *et al.* [20]. Pradhan and Chakraverty [21] studied the static analysis of functionally graded rectangular plates. The modified finite element-transfer matrix method has been proposed for static analysis of structures by Ozturk *et al.* [22]. Mata *et al.* [23] studied the static analysis of beam structures. Hierarchical models have been presented by Giunta *et al.* [24] for the static analysis of three-dimensional sandwich beam structures.

An ANN method for solving LSEs has been discussed in the following section.

6.2 ANN-Based Methodology

A linear system of equations may be written as

$$AX = B \text{ or } \sum_{j=1}^{n} a_{ij} x_j = b_i, i = 1, 2, \cdots, n \qquad (6.1)$$

where $A = [a_{ij}]$ is a $n \times n$ matrix, $X = [x_1, x_2, \cdots, x_n]^T$ and $B = [b_1, b_2, \cdots, b_n]^T$ are $n \times 1$ unknown and known vectors, respectively.

A single-layer ANN model has been constructed in Fig. 6.1 to handle LSEs. From Eq. (6.1), $A_i = [a_{i_1}, a_{i_2}, \cdots, a_{i_n}]^T$ and b_i ($i = 1, 2, \cdots, n$) are chosen as the input and target output, respectively. Here, x_j ($j = 1, 2, \cdots, n$) are the weights of the ANN architecture. Taking the input, target output and weights, the ANN model is trained until the weight vector x_j converges to the desired solution or the error is minimized.

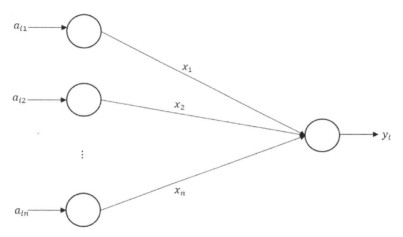

Fig. 6.1. Single-layer ANN model.

ANN output of the model (Fig. 6.1) is given by

$$y_i = g\left(\sum_{j=1}^{n} a_{ij} x_j\right), \quad i = 1, 2, \cdots, n \tag{6.2}$$

where g is the activation function. Here, the activation function is chosen to be identity.

The error is calculated as

$$e_i = b_i - y_i \tag{6.3}$$

Further, the sum squared error is

$$E = \frac{1}{2} \sum_{i=1}^{n} e_i^2 \tag{6.4}$$

Weights of the architecture are adjusted using the steepest descent algorithm as

$$\Delta x_j = -\eta \frac{\partial E}{\partial x_j} = -\eta \frac{\partial E}{\partial e_i} \frac{\partial e_i}{\partial y_i} \frac{\partial y_i}{\partial x_j} = \eta \sum_{i=1}^{n} e_i a_{ij} \qquad (6.5)$$

and the updated weight vector is

$$X^{(k+1)} = X^{(k)} + \Delta x_j, \; j = 1, 2, \cdots, n \qquad (6.6)$$

where η is the learning parameter and $X^{(k)}$ is the kth updated weight vector.

Algorithm:

Step 1: Choose the precision tolerance '*tol*', learning parameter η, random weights, $k = 0$ and $E = 0$;

Step 2: Calculate $y_i = \sum_{j=1}^{n} a_{ij} x_j$, $e_i = b_i - y_i$;

Step 3: The sum squared error is calculated as $E = E + \dfrac{1}{2} \sum_{i=1}^{n} e_i^2$ and

weight updating formula is given by

$$X^{(k+1)} = X^{(k)} + \Delta x_j, \; j = 1, 2, \cdots, n \text{ where } \Delta x_j = \eta \sum_{i=1}^{n} e_i a_{ij}$$

If $E < tol$, then go to Step 2, else go to Step 4.

Step 4: Print X.

6.3 Numerical Examples

Five LSEs having different dimensions viz. 3×3, 4×4, 6×6, 10×10 and 5×5 have been solved in Examples 6.1, 6.2, 6.3, 6.4 and 6.5, respectively. An ANN method (Section 6.2) is used to solve these systems. Further, Example 6.5 has been solved to show the efficacy of the ANN approach over existing numerical methods. Convergence plots/tables for the different examples have also been illustrated.

Example 6.1: Let us consider a linear system

$$4x_1 - 2x_2 + 7x_3 = 12$$

$$7x_1 + 6x_2 - 3x_3 = 15 \qquad (6.7)$$

$$2x_1 + 8x_2 - 5x_3 = 18$$

where the solution is $x_1 = 1.6337$, $x_2 = 1.1485$ and $x_3 = 1.1089$.

The ANN procedure is applied to solve the system (6.7). Here, the initial weights are randomly chosen as 0.1, 0.1 and 0.1 with learning parameter 0.009 to get the converged solution 1.6337, 1.1485 and 1.1089, respectively. Successive simulation results of the solution with respect to different tolerance criteria have been included in Table 6.1. Further, the convergence plot of the solution has been shown in Fig. 6.2.

Table 6.1. Convergence table of the solution for Eq. (6.7).

	$E < 10^{-1}$	$E < 10^{-3}$	$E < 10^{-6}$	$E < 10^{-9}$
x_1	1.5957	1.6300	1.6335	1.6337
x_2	1.1743	1.1509	1.1486	1.1485
x_3	1.1176	1.1097	1.1089	1.1089

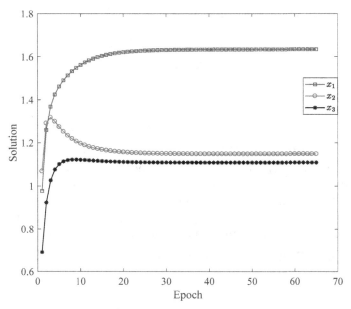

Fig. 6.2. Convergence plot of the solution for system (6.7).

Example 6.2: Further, another linear system is considered as follows:

$$2x_1 - 3x_2 + x_3 + 2x_4 = 7$$

$$-x_1 + x_2 + 3x_3 + 3x_4 = 5 \qquad (6.8)$$

$$3x_1 - x_3 + 4x_4 = 24$$

$$5x_1 + 3x_2 + 2x_3 - x_4 = 5$$

where the solution is $x_1 = 2$, $x_2 = 1$, $x_3 = -2$ and $x_4 = 4$.

The ANN procedure is implemented to solve the system (6.8). Accordingly, the ANN architecture is trained with arbitrary weights to get the desired solution as (2, 1, −2, 4). Here, the learning parameter is considered as 0.01. Table 6.2 includes the simulation result of the solution with respect to different tolerance criteria. The convergence plot of the solution has been depicted in Fig. 6.3.

Table 6.2. Convergence table of the solution for Eq. (6.8).

	$E < 10^{-1}$	$E < 10^{-3}$	$E < 10^{-7}$	$E < 10^{-10}$
x_1	2.0178	2.0018	2.0000	2.0000
x_2	0.9107	0.9911	0.9999	1.0000
x_3	-1.9059	-1.9907	-1.9999	-2.0000
x_4	3.9486	3.9949	3.9999	4.0000

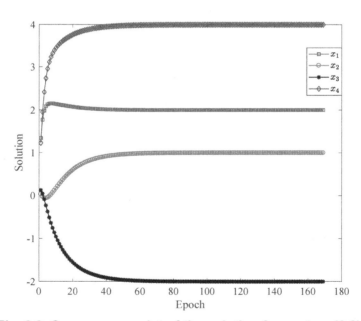

Fig. 6.3. Convergence plot of the solution for system (6.8).

It may be seen from Fig. 6.3 that the solution starts converging as we increase the number of epochs.

Example 6.3: In the following example, a 6×6 system has been considered

$$\begin{bmatrix} 8 & 5 & -11 & 8 & -4 & 11 \\ 2 & 9 & 7 & -11 & 5 & -8 \\ -9 & 7 & -2 & 12 & -5 & 6 \\ 11 & -9 & 11 & 2 & 9 & 0 \\ 7 & 10 & -4 & -3 & 8 & -6 \\ 4 & -7 & -6 & -8 & 7 & 10 \end{bmatrix} \begin{bmatrix} x_1 \\ x_2 \\ x_3 \\ x_4 \\ x_5 \\ x_6 \end{bmatrix} = \begin{bmatrix} 32 \\ 29 \\ -24 \\ 28 \\ -26 \\ 27 \end{bmatrix} \qquad (6.9)$$

where the solution is $[3.6264; 1.4489; 4.0145; -3.4745; -4.0068; 4.6975]^T$.

An ANN algorithm has been applied to solve Eq. (6.9) by taking the random weights. The learning parameter is chosen as 0.002. In this case, the final solution is computed as $[3.6264; 1.4489; 4.0145; -3.4745; -4.0068; 4.6975]^T$. Simulation result and the convergence plot of the solution have been shown in Table 6.3 and Fig. 6.4, respectively.

Table 6.3. Convergence table of the solution for Eq. (6.9).

	$E < 10^{-1}$	$E < 10^{-3}$	$E < 10^{-5}$	$E < 10^{-7}$
x_1	3.6051	3.6243	3.6262	3.6264
x_2	1.4312	1.4471	1.4487	1.4489
x_3	3.9811	4.0111	4.0142	4.0145
x_4	-3.4492	-3.4720	-3.4743	-3.4745
x_5	-3.9644	-4.0025	-4.0064	-4.0068
x_6	4.6672	4.6944	4.6972	4.6975

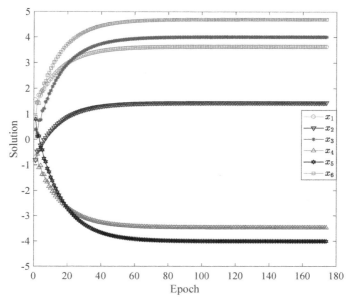

Fig. 6.4. Convergence plot of the solution for system (6.9).

Example 6.4: Let us consider a 10×10 system

$$
\begin{bmatrix}
20 & 1 & -8 & 6 & -5 & 4 & 3 & -2 & -5 & 1 \\
2 & 5 & 6 & -11 & 5 & 8 & -2 & 5 & -19 & -10 \\
5 & -2 & 1 & 11 & -14 & 5 & 2 & 3 & -9 & 12 \\
2 & -6 & 15 & 16 & 9 & 3 & -15 & 0 & 5 & 4 \\
0 & 3 & 6 & -4 & 2 & 17 & 15 & 5 & 13 & 2 \\
10 & -2 & 7 & -16 & 15 & -4 & 3 & 12 & 0 & -1 \\
12 & 2 & -6 & 1 & 5 & 8 & 2 & 5 & -9 & 0 \\
5 & 2 & 1 & -1 & 0 & 15 & 12 & 3 & -19 & -2 \\
-2 & 9 & 0 & 6 & 19 & -13 & 5 & 4 & -5 & -14 \\
5 & -13 & 16 & 14 & 1 & 7 & -8 & 5 & 3 & 6
\end{bmatrix}
\begin{bmatrix}
x_1 \\ x_2 \\ x_3 \\ x_4 \\ x_5 \\ x_6 \\ x_7 \\ x_8 \\ x_9 \\ x_{10}
\end{bmatrix}
=
\begin{bmatrix}
60 \\ 39 \\ 45 \\ 35 \\ 55 \\ 38 \\ 59 \\ 48 \\ 41 \\ 46
\end{bmatrix}
\quad (6.10)
$$

where the solution is $[3.7440; 3.4696; 2.5514; 1.0844; 0.2155; 0.1039; 0.8289; 3.5354; -0.0126; 0.7383]^T$.

System (6.10) is solved using the ANN method. The initial weights are randomly chosen to obtain the desired solution whose corresponding convergence plot can be visualized in Fig. 6.5. The learning parameter is taken as 0.0002.

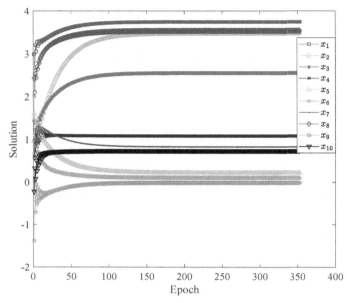

Fig. 6.5. Convergence plot of the solution for system (6.10).

It is quite evident from this example that the ANN method is useful in systems having higher dimensions. Further, the next example has been solved using the ANN procedure which may not be solved by both Jacobi and Gauss–Seidel methods.

Example 6.5: The following LSEs are considered

$$\begin{bmatrix} 2 & -3 & 1 & 7 & 1 \\ 2 & 8 & -4 & 5 & -1 \\ 1 & 3 & -3 & 0 & 5 \\ -5 & 2 & 3 & 4 & 1 \\ 4 & 2 & 7 & 4 & 0 \end{bmatrix}\begin{bmatrix} x_1 \\ x_2 \\ x_3 \\ x_4 \\ x_5 \end{bmatrix} = \begin{bmatrix} 14 \\ -1 \\ 4 \\ -19 \\ 5 \end{bmatrix} \qquad (6.11)$$

which may not be solved using both Jacobi and Gauss–Seidel methods.

System (6.11) may not be solved using both Jacobi and Gauss–Seidel method because the system is not diagonally dominant. Instead, ANN procedure is applied to solve the system to get the desired result. Here, the initial weights may be considered as $[0.25; 0.15; 0.12; 0.35; 0.30]^T$ along with learning parameter 0.003 to obtain the converged solution as $[3.1289; -1.5775; -0.8939; 0.4742; 0.5844]^T$. The simulation result of the solution with respect to different tolerance criteria has been given in Table 6.4. The convergence plot of the solution has been shown in Fig. 6.6.

Table 6.4. Convergence table of the solution for Eq. (6.11).

	$E < 10^{-1}$	$E < 10^{-3}$	$E < 10^{-5}$	$E < 10^{-8}$
x_1	3.1128	3.1277	3.1288	3.1289
x_2	-1.5598	-1.5754	-1.5772	-1.5775
x_3	-0.8792	-0.8922	-0.8937	-0.8939
x_4	0.4651	0.4729	0.4740	0.4742
x_5	0.5749	0.5827	0.5841	0.5844

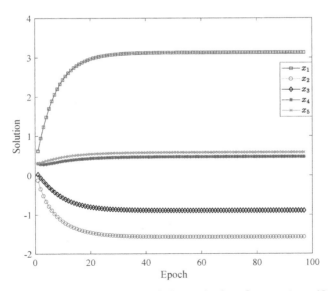

Fig. 6.6. Convergence plot of the solution for system (6.11).

Five examples of LSEs having different dimensions have been solved as above using the ANN method. An example has also been solved to show the advantage of the ANN technique over known numerical methods.

In the next section, an application of LSEs has been investigated using the ANN method. It is known that the static analysis of structures may in general be converted to LSEs. In this regard, a three-bar truss problem has been considered next.

6.4 Static Structural Problem

A three-bar truss structure [25] has been depicted in Fig. 6.7. The horizontal u^j ($j = 1, 3, 5$) and vertical u^j ($j = 2, 4, 6$) displacements have been considered. External load is acting on node 3. The variables such as length of the three sections, cross-sectional areas and Young's modulus have been taken as $l^{(1)} = 800$ mm, $l^{(2)} = l^{(3)} = 400\sqrt{2}$ mm, $A^{(1)} = 1500$ mm^2, $A^{(2)} = A^{(3)} = 2000$ mm^2 and $E^{(i)} = 800$ Gpa ($i = 1, 2, 3$), respectively. External load is chosen as $F = 150$ kN. The static responses have been found using the ANN algorithm.

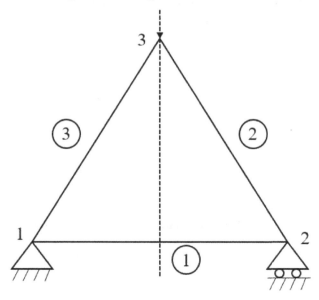

Fig. 6.7. Three-bar truss structure [25].

The static analysis of three-bar truss structures leads to LSEs. As such, the LSEs can be obtained as [25]

$$\begin{bmatrix} 728.55 & -353.55 & 353.55 \\ -353.55 & 707.10 & 0 \\ 353.55 & 0 & 707.10 \end{bmatrix} \begin{bmatrix} \delta_3 \\ \delta_5 \\ \delta_6 \end{bmatrix} = \begin{bmatrix} 0 \\ 0 \\ -150 \end{bmatrix} \tag{6.12}$$

The ANN procedure is applied to solve the system (6.12). The final solution has been obtained as $[0.2; \ 0.1; \ -0.312]^T$ by starting with arbitrary weights. For this problem, the learning parameter is selected as 0.0000009. The convergence plot of the solution can be visualized as Fig. 6.8.

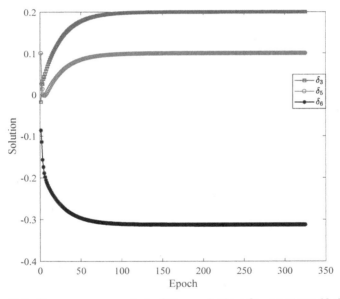

Fig. 6.8. Convergence plot of the solution for system (6.12).

The result obtained using the ANN procedure is in good agreement with the result given in Bhavikatti [25].

6.5 Conclusion

An ANN-based procedure with step-by-step algorithm has been included in this chapter for solving LSEs. Different examples have been solved to validate the ANN method. An example has also been solved to show the advantage of the ANN method over existing numerical methods viz. Jacobi and Gauss–Seidel. Moreover, an application of static structural problem has been solved. Finally, convergence plots/tables for different example problems have also been illustrated.

References

[1] A. Cichocki and R. Unbehauen, (1992). Neural networks for solving systems of linear equations and related problems. *IEEE Transactions on Circuits and Systems I Fundamental Theory and Applications, 39*(2), 124–138.

[2] J. Wang, (1992). Electronic realisation of recurrent neural network for solving simultaneous linear equations. *Electronics Letters, 28*(5), 493–495.

[3] L. A. V. De Carvalho and V. C. Barbosa, (1992). Fast linear system solution by neural networks. *Operations research letters, 11*(3), 141–145.

[4] J. Wang and H. Li, (1994). Solving simultaneous linear equations using recurrent neural networks. *Information Sciences, 76*(3–4), 255–277.

[5] H. B. Li and F. H. Shang, (2007). Neural network method in solving illconditioned linear system of equations. *Journal of Liaoning Technical University, 6*.

[6] S. A. Rahman and M. S. Ansari, (2011). A neural circuit with transcendental energy function for solving system of linear equations. *Analog Integrated Circuits and Signal Processing, 66*(3), 433–440.

[7] S. Mall, S. K. Jeswal, and S. Chakraverty, (2020). Connectionist learning models for application problems involving differential and integral equations. *Mathematical Methods in Interdisciplinary Sciences*, 1–22.

[8] H. Anton and C. Rorres, (2013). *Elementary linear algebra: Applications version*. John Wiley & Sons.

[9] K. E. Atkinson, (2008). *An Introduction to Numerical Analysis.* John wiley & sons.

[10] A. S. Householder, (2006). *Principles of Numerical Analysis.* Courier Corporation.

[11] E. Süli and D. F. Mayers, (2003). *An Introduction to Numerical Analysis.* Cambridge university press.

[12] A. G. Striz, C. Weilong, and C. W. Bert, (1994). Static analysis of structures by the quadrature element method (QEM). *International Journal of Solids and Structures, 31*(20), 2807–2818.

[13] X. Wang and H. Gu, (1997). Static analysis of frame structures by the differential quadrature element method. *International Journal for Numerical Methods in Engineering, 40*(4), 759–772.

[14] X. Wang, Y. L. Wang, and R. B. Chen, (1998). Static and free vibrational analysis of rectangular plates by the differential quadrature element method. *Communications in Numerical Methods in Engineering, 14*(12), 1133–1141.

[15] S. Z. Feng, X. Y. Cui, F. Chen, S. Z. Liu, and D. Y. Meng, (2016). An edge/face-based smoothed radial point interpolation method for static analysis of structures. *Engineering Analysis with Boundary Elements, 68*, 1–10.

[16] M. Such, J. R. Jimenez-Octavio, A. Carnicero, and O. Lopez-Garcia, (2009). An approach based on the catenary equation to deal with static analysis of three dimensional cable structures. *Engineering Structures, 31*(9), 2162–2170.

[17] E. Viola, F. Tornabene, E. Ferretti, and N. Fantuzzi, (2013). On static analysis of composite plane state structures via GDQFEM and cell method. *CMES, 94*(5), 421–458.

[18] C. Franciosi, and S. Tomasiello, (2004). A modified quadrature element method to perform static analysis of structures. *International Journal of Mechanical Sciences, 46*(6), 945–959.

[19] C. D. Crane III, J. Duffy, and J. C. Correa, (2005). Static analysis of tensegrity structures. *J. Mech. Des., 127*(2), 257–268.

[20] S. Zghal, A. Frikha, and F. Dammak, (2017). Static analysis of functionally graded carbon nanotube-reinforced plate and shell structures. *Composite Structures, 176*, 1107–1123.

[21] K. K. Pradhan and S. Chakraverty, (2015). Static analysis of functionally graded thin rectangular plates with various boundary supports. *Archives of Civil and Mechanical Engineering, 15*(3), 721–734.

[22] D. Ozturk, K. Bozdogan, and A. Nuhoglu, (2012). Modified finite element-transfer matrix method for the static analysis of structures. *Structural Engineering and Mechanics, 43*(6), 761–769.

[23] P. Mata, S. Oller, and A. H. Barbat, (2007). Static analysis of beam structures under nonlinear geometric and constitutive behavior. *Computer Methods in Applied Mechanics and Engineering, 196*(45–48), 4458–4478.

[24] G. Giunta, S. Belouettar, H. Nasser, E. H. Kiefer-Kamal, and T. Thielen, (2015). Hierarchical models for the static analysis of three-dimensional sandwich beam structures. *Composite Structures, 133*, 1284–1301.

[25] S. S. Bhavikatti, (2005). *Finite Element Analysis*. New Age International.

7

Systems of Nonlinear Equations in Electrical Network Analysis

A novel ANN model for solving systems of nonlinear equations has been discussed in this chapter. Three numerical examples of nonlinear systems have been solved using the ANN method. Moreover, an application problem of electrical network analysis has been investigated to show the efficiency of the ANN method. Finally, convergence plots of the solutions for the solved problems have also been illustrated.

7.1 Introduction

Nonlinear system of equations consists of a set of simultaneous nonlinear equations. Nonlinear systems have different applications such as in electrical network analysis, triangulation of GPS signals, fluid flow problems, etc. There exist limited numerical methods such as Newton's [1], Broyden's [2], etc. for solving nonlinear systems. As such, this chapter deals with an ANN-based approach for handling nonlinear systems.

There are different approaches available in the literature for solving systems of nonlinear equations. In this context, Ahmad *et al.* [3] proposed a multi-step Newton method for solving nonlinear systems. A Jacobi-type block Broyden algorithm has been discussed by Yang *et al.* [4]. Shi [5] presented a novel globalization procedure for solving a nonlinear system of equations. A multipoint iterative method has been developed by Lotfi *et al.* [6]. Grosan and Abraham [7] solved nonlinear systems by viewing them as a multiobjective optimization problem. A Soccer League Competition algorithm has been introduced by Moosavian and Roodsari [8]. Invasive weed optimization technique has been used by Pourjafari and Mojallali [9] for solving nonlinear systems. Luo *et al.* [10] presented a chaos optimization and quasi-Newton method for nonlinear systems. Two new two-step iterative methods have been presented by Noor and Waseem [11]. Jafari and Daftardar-Gejji [12] discussed a revised version of adomian decomposition method (ADM) for nonlinear systems. Deflation algorithm for computing multiple roots of a nonlinear system has been proposed by Ojika *et al.* [13]. Babolian *et al.* [14] applied the ADM method for solving nonlinear systems. Numerical algorithms based on Newton's method have been developed by Abbasbandy [15]. A combination of nonlinear ABS methods and quasi-Newton methods has been proposed by Galantai and Jeney [16]. Mourrain and Pavone [17] discussed a subdivision method to solve systems of polynomial equations. A homotopy algorithm for solving polynomial systems has been introduced by Dedieu *et al.* [18].

A nonlinear system is a combination of two or more nonlinear equations as follows:

$$
\begin{aligned}
F_1(x_1, x_2, \cdots, x_n) &= d_1 \\
F_2(x_1, x_2, \cdots, x_n) &= d_2 \\
&\vdots \\
F_n(x_1, x_2, \cdots, x_n) &= d_n
\end{aligned}
\tag{7.1}
$$

where x_i ($i = 1, 2, \cdots, n$) are unknown variables, F_i ($i = 1, 2, \cdots, n$) are nonlinear real functions of x_i and d_i ($i = 1, 2, \cdots, n$) are the constant terms.

7.2 Numerical Examples

Three numerical examples of systems of nonlinear equations have been solved using the ANN procedure (Section 5.2.1, Chapter 5) in this section. Detailed ANN architecture with few steps for solving example 7.1 has been discussed. Further, convergence plots for the solved examples have also been shown for clear understanding.

Example 7.1: Let us consider a system of nonlinear equations as follows:

$$x_1^2 + x_2^2 + x_3^2 = 6$$
$$x_1^2 - x_2^2 + 2x_3^2 = 2 \qquad (7.2)$$
$$2x_1^2 + x_2^2 - x_3^2 = 3$$

which has a solution $(1, \sqrt{3}, \sqrt{2})$.

The network architecture for Eq. (7.2) has been constructed in Fig. 7.1.

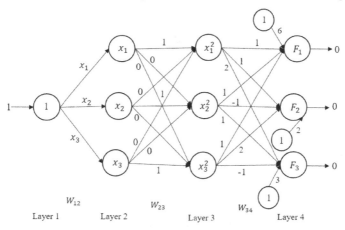

Fig. 7.1. ANN architecture for Eq. (7.2).

The ANN model for Eq. (7.2) has been shown in Fig. 7.1. This model consists of four layers, that is Layer 1 (input layer), Layers 2 and 3 (hidden layers) and Layer 4 (output layer). The input layer consists of one linear unit node with a constant input equal to unity. Further, the first hidden layer (Layer 2) has three nodes for the linear terms x_1, x_2, x_3 and the next hidden layer comprises three nodes for quadratic terms. Finally, the output layer consists of three summation units whose total inputs are the expression of the left-hand side of the different individual equations of Eq. (7.2). It has been clearly shown in Fig. 7.1 that the weights from Layer 2 to Layer 3 are fixed depending upon the nonlinear system. Different coefficients of Eq. (7.2) are taken as the weights between Layers 3 and 4. There are only variable weights joining Layer 1 to Layer 2, which is nothing but the solution of the considered system. There are also bias nodes connecting to the output nodes and W_{ij} denotes the weights between the layers i and j.

Various weight matrices between the layers are given as follows:

$$W_{12} = \begin{bmatrix} W_{12}^{(1)} \\ W_{12}^{(2)} \\ W_{12}^{(3)} \end{bmatrix} = \begin{bmatrix} x_1 \\ x_2 \\ x_3 \end{bmatrix}$$

$$W_{23} = \begin{bmatrix} W_{23}^{(11)} & W_{23}^{(12)} & W_{23}^{(13)} \\ W_{23}^{(21)} & W_{23}^{(22)} & W_{23}^{(23)} \\ W_{23}^{(31)} & W_{23}^{(32)} & W_{23}^{(33)} \end{bmatrix} = \begin{bmatrix} 1 & 0 & 0 \\ 0 & 1 & 0 \\ 0 & 0 & 1 \end{bmatrix}$$

$$W_{34} = \begin{bmatrix} W_{34}^{(11)} & W_{34}^{(12)} & W_{34}^{(13)} \\ W_{34}^{(21)} & W_{34}^{(22)} & W_{34}^{(23)} \\ W_{34}^{(31)} & W_{34}^{(32)} & W_{34}^{(33)} \end{bmatrix} = \begin{bmatrix} 1 & 1 & 1 \\ 1 & -1 & 2 \\ 2 & 1 & -1 \end{bmatrix}$$

where the subscripts 1, 2, 3, 4 denote the different layers of the ANN architecture.

Now, Eq. (7.2) has been solved using the ANN method. Accordingly, the ANN architecture is trained with arbitrary weights (0.1, 0.2, 0.3) and learning parameter 0.1 to get the final converged solution as (1, 1.7321, 1.4142). The convergence plot of the solution can be visualized in Fig. 7.2.

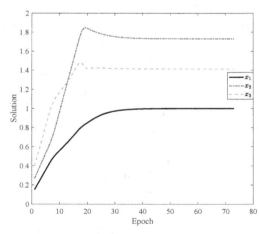

Fig. 7.2. Convergence plot of the solution for Eq. (7.2).

Example 7.2: A nonlinear system of equations has been considered

$$2x_1^4 + x_2^4 - x_3^4 - x_1^2 = -102$$
$$4x_1^4 + 3x_2^4 + x_3^4 + x_2^3 = 584 \qquad (7.3)$$
$$-x_1^4 + x_2^4 + 2x_3^4 - x_3^3 = 368$$

which has a solution (3, 1, 4).

The ANN procedure has been applied to solve Eq. (7.3). In this case, starting with initial weights (0.5, 0.5, 0.6) and learning parameter 0.002, we obtain the final converged solution as (3, 1, 4). Figure 7.3 shows the convergence plot of the solution where one may see that the solution starts converging as we increase the number of epochs.

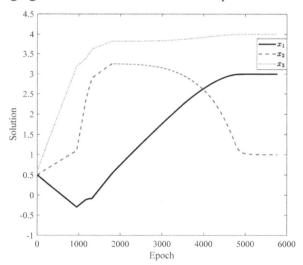

Fig. 7.3. Convergence plot of the solution for Eq. (7.3).

Example 7.3: Further, a nonlinear system has been considered

$$x_1^2 + x_2^2 + x_3^2 = 14$$
$$2x_2^2 + x_3^2 = 19 \qquad (7.4)$$
$$2x_1^2 + x_3^2 = 9$$

which has a solution (2, 3, 1).

The ANN method has been implemented to solve Eq. (7.4). Let us consider the initial weights and learning parameter as (0.4, 0.6, 0.2) and 0.02, respectively, for this problem. The solution may be obtained as (2, 3, 1) whose convergence plot may be seen in Fig. 7.4.

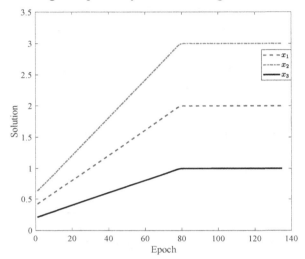

Fig. 7.4. Convergence plot of the solution for Eq. (7.4).

This section investigates three numerical examples of systems of nonlinear equations. ANN may be helpful in solving these systems. The ANN results obtained for Eqs. (7.2), (7.3) and (7.4) may be verified by putting these in the corresponding equations, respectively. Further, an application problem of nonlinear systems has been examined in the following section.

7.3 Application Problem

An electrical circuit analysis problem [19] in two variables has been considered in this section. The circuit comprises two tunnel diodes, a resistor and a voltage source connected in series. The voltage across the diodes is denoted as x_1 and x_2. Accordingly, the circuit design equations are given by [19]

$$30 - 13.3(2.5x_1^3 - 10.5x_1^2 + 11.8x_1) - x_1 - x_2 = 0$$
$$2.5x_1^3 - 10.5x_1^2 + 11.8x_1 - 0.43x_2^3 + 2.69x_2^2 - 4.5x_2 = 0$$

(7.5)

Here, the operating points of the circuit have to be determined.

Equation (7.5) may further be simplified as

$$-33.25x_1^3 + 139.65x_1^2 - 157.94x_1 - x_2 + 30 = 0$$
$$2.5x_1^3 - 10.5x_1^2 + 11.8x_1 - 0.43x_2^3 + 2.69x_2^2 - 4.5x_2 = 0$$

(7.6)

System (7.6) has been solved using the ANN method. Here, we have selected the initial weights and learning parameter as (0.3, 0.2) and 0.001, respectively. As such, the solution has been found as (1.6675, 0.7750) whose convergence plot has been illustrated in Fig. 7.5.

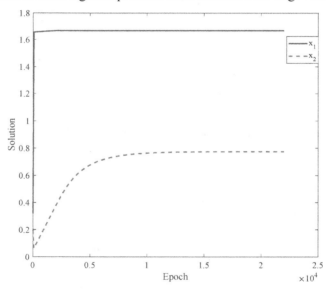

Fig. 7.5. Convergence plot of the solution for Eq. (7.6).

7.4 Conclusion

This chapter addresses a novel ANN-based technique for solving systems of nonlinear equations. ANN is an alternative and efficient method in solving systems of nonlinear equations. The efficiency of the ANN method has been verified by solving three nonlinear systems. Further, an application problem of systems of nonlinear equations has been investigated. Finally, convergence plots of the solutions for the solved problems have also been depicted.

References

[1] C. T. Kelley, (2003). *Solving nonlinear equations with Newton's method* (Vol. 1). Siam.

[2] D. M. Gay and R. B. Schnabel, (1978). Solving systems of nonlinear equations by Broyden's method with projected updates. In *Nonlinear Programming 3* (pp. 245–281). Academic Press.

[3] F. Ahmad, E. Tohidi, and J. A. Carrasco, (2016). A parameterized multi-step Newton method for solving systems of nonlinear equations. *Numerical Algorithms, 71*(3), 631–653.

[4] G. Yang, L. C. Dutto, and M. Fortin, (1997). Inexact Block Jacobi--Broyden methods for solving nonlinear systems of equations. *SIAM Journal on Scientific Computing, 18*(5), 1367–1392.

[5] Y. Shi, (1996). A globalization procedure for solving nonlinear systems of equations. *Numerical Algorithms, 12*(2), 273–286.

[6] T. Lotfi, P. Bakhtiari, A. Cordero, K. Mahdiani, and J. R. Torregrosa, (2015). Some new efficient multipoint iterative methods for solving nonlinear systems of equations. *International Journal of Computer Mathematics, 92*(9), 1921–1934.

[7] C. Grosan and A. Abraham, (2008). A new approach for solving nonlinear equations systems. *IEEE Transactions on Systems, Man, and Cybernetics-Part A: Systems and Humans, 38*(3), 698–714.

[8] N. Moosavian and B. K. Roodsari, (2013). Soccer league competition algorithm, a new method for solving systems of nonlinear equations. *International Journal of Intelligence Science, 4*(01), 7.

[9] E. Pourjafari and H. Mojallali, (2012). Solving nonlinear equations systems with a new approach based on invasive weed optimization algorithm and clustering. *Swarm and Evolutionary Computation, 4*, 33–43.

[10] Y. Z. Luo, G. J. Tang, and L. N. Zhou, (2008). Hybrid approach for solving systems of nonlinear equations using chaos optimization and quasi-Newton method. *Applied Soft Computing, 8*(2), 1068–1073.

[11] M. A. Noor and M. Waseem, (2009). Some iterative methods for solving a system of nonlinear equations. *Computers & Mathematics with Applications, 57*(1), 101–106.

[12] H. Jafari and V. Daftardar-Gejji (2006). Revised Adomian decomposition method for solving a system of nonlinear equations. *Applied Mathematics and Computation, 175*(1), 1–7.

[13] T. Ojika, S. Watanabe, and T. Mitsui, (1983). Deflation algorithm for the multiple roots of a system of nonlinear equations. *Journal of mathematical analysis and applications, 96*(2), 463–479.

[14] E. Babolian, J. Biazar, and A. R. Vahidi, (2004). Solution of a system of nonlinear equations by Adomian decomposition method. *Applied Mathematics and Computation, 150*(3), 847–854.

[15] S. Abbasbandy (2005). Extended Newton's method for a system of nonlinear equations by modified Adomian decomposition method. *Applied Mathematics and Computation, 170*(1), 648–656.

[16] A. Galantai and A. Jeney, (1996). Quasi-Newton ABS methods for solving nonlinear algebraic systems of equations. *Journal of Optimization Theory and Applications, 89*(3), 561–573.

[17] B. Mourrain and J. P. Pavone, (2009). Subdivision methods for solving polynomial equations. *Journal of Symbolic Computation, 44*(3), 292–306.

[18] J. P. Dedieu, G. Malajovich, and M. Shub, (2013). Adaptive step-size selection for homotopy methods to solve polynomial equations. *IMA Journal of Numerical Analysis, 33*(1), 1–29.

[19] M. Arounassalame (2012). Analysis of nonlinear electrical circuits using bernstein polynomials. *International Journal of Automation and Computing, 9*(1), 81–86.

8

Eigenvalue Problems with Application in Structural Dynamics

This chapter addresses a novel ANN-based technique for solving eigenvalue problems. The detailed ANN architecture has been shown for clear understanding. Firstly, two numerical examples of eigenvalue problems have been solved using the ANN method. In this regard, it is worth mentioning that the dynamic analysis of structures may lead to eigenvalue problems in general. As such, two application problems of structural dynamics have been solved using the ANN method. Convergence plots for the computed eigenvalues have also been included.

8.1 Introduction

Eigenvalue problems may arise in various situations while solving engineering and science problems. There are various traditional iterative methods such as power, inverse power, Rayleigh quotient, QR, etc. to find the eigenvalues. However, these methods have various limitations, for example, in some cases only the largest and smallest eigenvalues can be found and various other methods may depend on the matrix type. As such, we have discussed here an ANN method to find the real eigenvalues of an eigenvalue problem. Further, eigenvalue problems have various applications in vibrational analysis, geology, molecular orbitals, Schrödinger equation, etc.

Different traditional methods may be found in [1–6] to solve eigenvalue problems. Further, Sleijpen and Van der Vorst [7] proposed a Jacobi–Davidson iteration method for solving eigenvalue problems. There exist many other works related to eigenvalue problems but our target here is about the application of ANN method to eigenvalue problems. In this context, an ANN approach for solving the eigenvalue problem has been developed by Cichocki and Unbehauen [8]. Samardzija and Waterland [9] introduced an ANN method for computing real eigenvalues and eigenvectors. ANN-based technique for computing eigenvalues of symmetric matrix has been discussed by Yi *et al.* [10]. Feng *et al.* [11] presented a recurrent neural network model for solving eigenvalue problems.

Sometimes, the dynamic analysis of structures reduces to eigenvalue problems. In this regard, Bui *et al.* [12] proposed a moving Kriging interpolation-based element-free Galerkin method for dynamic analysis of two-dimensional solids. An adaptive finite element technique has been developed by Kuan-Jung and Wilson [13] for dynamic analysis of structures. Boundary element method has been used by Providakis and Beskos [14] for dynamic analysis of beams. Moghadas and Gholizadeh [15] introduced a novel wavelet backpropagation neural network for structural dynamics. An ANN procedure with detailed architecture has been proposed by Jeswal and Chakraverty [16] for structural dynamics problems.

Eigenvalue problem [4]: Given a matrix A of dimension $m \times m$, find a scalar λ and a non-zero vector x such that

$$Ax = \lambda x \tag{8.1}$$

where, λ is the eigenvalue and x is the corresponding eigenvector. The eigenvalues may be both real and complex.

The characteristic polynomial of Eq. (8.1) can be computed as

$$\det(\lambda I - A) = 0$$

Further, the above equation reduces to

$$a_1\lambda + a_2\lambda^2 + \cdots + a_n\lambda^n = c \tag{8.2}$$

where, $a_i \, (i = 1, 2, \cdots, n)$ are the different coefficients and c is the constant term.

8.2 ANN Model for Solving Eigenvalue Problems

ANN model for solving Eq. (8.2) is depicted in Fig. 8.1.

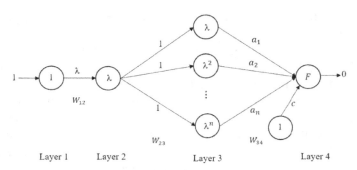

Fig. 8.1. ANN architecture for eigenvalue problems.

Generalized architecture for solving eigenvalue problems has been constructed in Fig. 8.1 comprising of four layers, Layer 1 (input layer), Layers 2 and 3 (hidden layers) and Layer 4 (output layer). The input layer consists of one linear unit node with a constant input equal to unity. Further, first hidden layer (Layer 2) has one node for the linear term λ and Layer 3 comprises a number of nodes depending upon the characteristic Eq. (8.2). Finally, the output layer consists of summation units whose total input is the expression of the left-hand side of Eq. (8.2). It may be shown in Fig. 8.1 that weights from Layers 2 to 3 are fixed, that is unity. Different coefficients of Eq. (8.2) are considered as the weights between Layers 3 and 4. There is only variable weight joining Layer 1 to 2, which is the solution (eigenvalue) of the given Eq. (8.2). There is also a bias node connecting to the output node and W_{ij} denotes the weights between the layers i and j. Further, the weights are written in vector form as

$$W_{12} = [W_{12}^{(1)}] = [\lambda]$$

$$W_{23} = \begin{bmatrix} W_{23}^{(11)} \\ W_{23}^{(21)} \\ \vdots \\ W_{23}^{(n1)} \end{bmatrix} = \begin{bmatrix} 1 \\ 1 \\ \vdots \\ 1 \end{bmatrix}$$

$$W_{34} = \begin{bmatrix} W_{34}^{(11)} \\ W_{34}^{(21)} \\ \vdots \\ W_{34}^{(n1)} \end{bmatrix} = \begin{bmatrix} a_1 \\ a_2 \\ \vdots \\ a_n \end{bmatrix}$$

where the subscripts 1, 2, 3, 4 denote the different layers of the ANN model.

8.3 Numerical Examples

Two numerical examples of eigenvalue problems have been addressed in this section. The ANN procedure (Section 3.2.1, Chapter 3) is applied to solve the problem. Convergence plots for the computed eigenvalues have also been depicted.

Example 8.1: Find the eigenvalues of the matrix

$$\begin{bmatrix} 4 & 1 & 2 & -1 \\ 2 & 0 & 1 & 2 \\ 3 & 1 & 4 & 5 \\ 0 & 1 & 6 & 3 \end{bmatrix}$$

Characteristic polynomial for the above matrix is given by

$$\lambda^4 - 11\lambda^3 - \lambda^2 + 123\lambda + 44 = 0 \tag{8.3}$$

ANN procedure has been applied to solve Eq. (8.3) to find the four eigenvalues. Initial weights and learning parameters used in the ANN procedure have been included in Table 8.1. Computed eigenvalues have also been given in the last column of Table 8.1. Convergence plots of the eigenvalues have been shown in Figs. 8.2–8.5.

Table 8.1. Eigenvalues using ANN procedure.

	Initial Weight	Learning Parameter (η)	Eigenvalues (λ)
λ_1	-4	10^{-5}	-2.8240
λ_2	0.1	10^{-4}	-0.3610

| λ_3 | 2.7 | 10^{-5} | 4.4196 |
| λ_4 | 8 | 10^{-6} | 9.7653 |

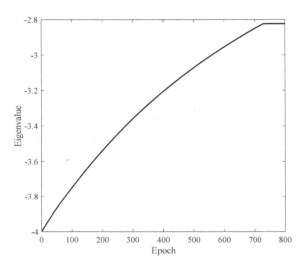

Fig. 8.2. First eigenvalue (-2.8240).

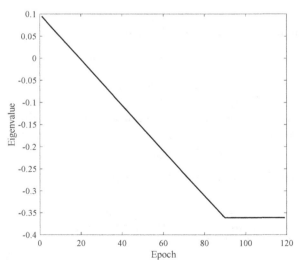

Fig. 8.3. Second eigenvalue (-0.3610).

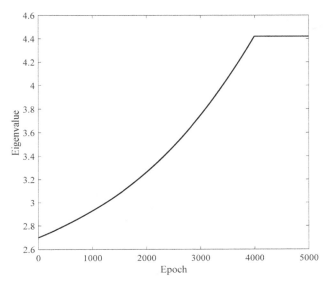

Fig. 8.4. Third eigenvalue (4.4196).

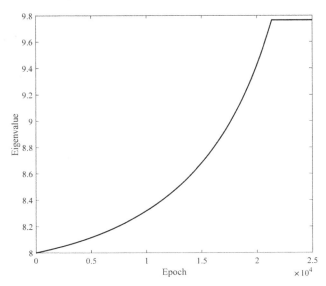

Fig. 8.5. Fourth eigenvalue (9.7653).

Example 8.2: Find the eigenvalues of the following matrix

$$A = \begin{bmatrix} 5 & 4 & 3 & 2 & 3 \\ 4 & 3 & 4 & 0 & 7 \\ 3 & 4 & 6 & -3 & 4 \\ 2 & 0 & -3 & 10 & -1 \\ 3 & 7 & 4 & -1 & 2 \end{bmatrix}$$

Characteristic polynomial for the above matrix is given by

$$\lambda^5 - 26\lambda^4 + 122\lambda^3 - 669\lambda^2 - 2128\lambda = -1405 \qquad (8.4)$$

Equation (8.4) has been solved using the ANN procedure to find the five eigenvalues. Table 8.2 includes the initial weights and learning parameters used in the ANN procedure to find the desired eigenvalues. Moreover, the computed eigenvalues have also been included in the last column of Table 8.2. The convergence plots of the eigenvalues have been illustrated in Figs. 8.6–8.10.

Table 8.2. Eigenvalues using ANN procedure.

	Initial Weight	Learning Parameter(η)	Eigenvalues (λ)
λ_1	-3.5	10^{-9}	-4.5807
λ_2	0.01	10^{-5}	1.0989
λ_3	1.3	10^{-5}	1.4835
λ_4	9	10^{-8}	11.2013
λ_5	15.4	10^{-9}	16.7970

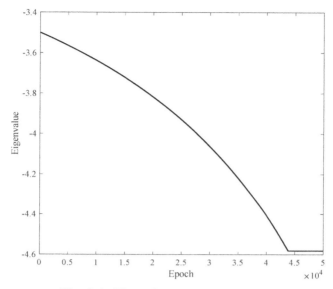

Fig. 8.6. First eigenvalue (-4.5807).

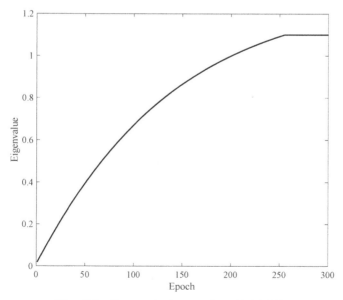

Fig. 8.7. Second eigenvalue (1.0989).

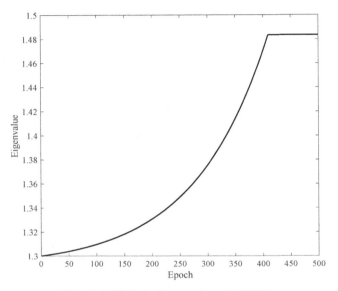

Fig. 8.8. Third eigenvalue (1.4835).

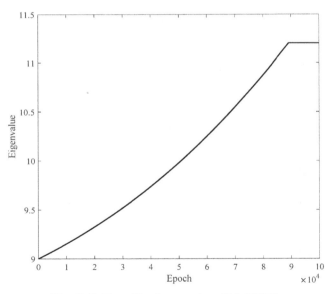

Fig. 8.9. Fourth eigenvalue (11.2013).

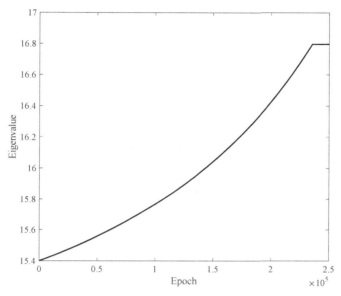

Fig. 8.10. Fifth eigenvalue (16.7970).

Dynamic analysis of structures may lead to eigenvalue problems. In this context, two application problems of structural dynamics viz. Four-degrees-of-freedom spring mass system and multi-storey shear structure have been investigated in the next section. The proposed ANN procedure (Section 3.2.1, Chapter 3) is applied to find the natural frequencies (eigenvalues) of the structural problems.

8.4 Application Problem

General equation for dynamic analysis of structure (free vibration) may be written as [17–21]

$$[M][\ddot{x}] + [C][\dot{x}] + [K][x] = 0 \qquad (8.5)$$

where $[M]$, $[C]$ and $[K]$ are the mass, damping and stiffness matrices, respectively.

The equation of motion in equilibrium situation can be obtained as

$$[M][\ddot{x}] + [K][x] = 0 \qquad (8.6)$$

where

$$M = \begin{bmatrix} m_1 & 0 & 0 & \cdots & 0 \\ 0 & m_2 & 0 & \cdots & 0 \\ \cdots & \cdots & \ddots & \cdots & \cdots \\ 0 & \cdots & 0 & m_{n-1} & 0 \\ 0 & \cdots & \cdots & 0 & m_n \end{bmatrix}, K = \begin{bmatrix} k_1 + k_2 & -k_2 & 0 & \cdots & 0 \\ -k_2 & k_2 + k_3 & -k_3 & \cdots & 0 \\ \cdots & \cdots & \ddots & \cdots & \cdots \\ 0 & \cdots & -k_{n-1} & k_{n-1} + k_n & k_n \\ 0 & \cdots & \cdots & -k_n & k_n \end{bmatrix}$$

Both sides of Eq. (8.6) can be multiplied with $[M]$ to get the following equation as (if inverse of M exists):

$$I\ddot{x} + M^{-1}Kx = 0 \qquad (8.7)$$

Putting $x = \phi e^{iwt}$ in Eq. (8.7), we have

$$Ax = \lambda x$$

where

$A = M^{-1}K$ (where A is a square matrix). $\qquad (8.8)$

8.4.1 Spring Mass System

A four-degrees-of-freedom spring mass system has been depicted in Fig. 8.11. The mass and stiffness parameters are chosen as $m_1 = 30\,\text{kg}$, $m_2 = 40\,\text{kg}$, $m_3 = 50\,\text{kg}$, $m_4 = 60\,\text{kg}$ and $k_1 = 200\,\text{N/m}$, $k_2 = 180\,\text{N/m}$, $k_3 = 160\,\text{N/m}$, $k_4 = 140\,\text{N/m}$, $k_5 = 120\,\text{N/m}$, respectively.

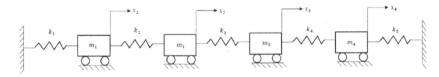

Fig. 8.11. Spring mass system with four degrees of freedom.

The mass and stiffness matrices may be calculated as

$$M = \begin{bmatrix} 40 & 0 & 0 & 0 \\ 0 & 50 & 0 & 0 \\ 0 & 0 & 60 & 0 \\ 0 & 0 & 0 & 70 \end{bmatrix} \text{ and } K = \begin{bmatrix} 380 & -180 & 0 & 0 \\ -180 & 340 & -160 & 0 \\ 0 & -160 & 300 & -140 \\ 0 & 0 & -140 & 260 \end{bmatrix}$$

From Eq. (8.8), the coefficient matrix may be computed as

$$A = M^{-1}K = \begin{bmatrix} 9.5000 & -4.5000 & 0 & 0 \\ -3.6000 & 6.8000 & -3.2000 & 0 \\ 0 & -2.6667 & 5.0000 & -2.3333 \\ 0 & 0 & -2.0000 & 3.7143 \end{bmatrix}$$

Characteristic polynomial for the above matrix is given by

$$\lambda^4 - 25.0143\lambda^3 + 195.8146\lambda^2 - 535.6586\lambda = -371.8875 \qquad (8.9)$$

ANN method is used to solve Eq. (8.9). The initial weights, learning parameter used in the ANN method along with the computed eigenvalues have been included in Table 8.3. Convergence plots of the eigenvalues have been illustrated in Figs. 8.12–8.15.

Table 8.3. Eigenvalues using ANN procedure.

	Initial Weight	Learning Parameter(η)	Eigenvalue
λ_1	0.01	10^{-5}	1.0382
λ_2	2.2	10^{-4}	3.8014
λ_3	6	10^{-4}	7.3444
λ_4	11	10^{-6}	12.8303

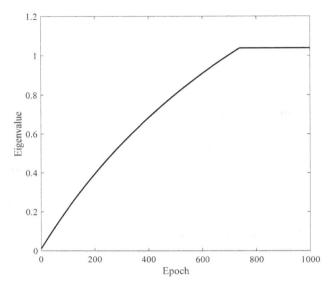

Fig. 8.12. First eigenvalue (1.0382).

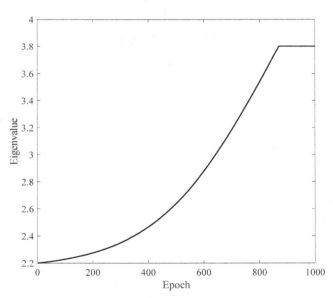

Fig. 8.13. Second eigenvalue (3.8014).

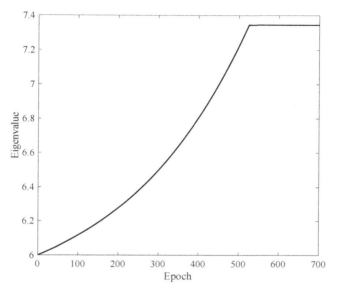

Fig. 8.14. Third eigenvalue (7.3444).

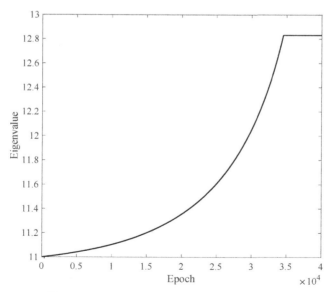

Fig. 8.15. Fourth eigenvalue (12.8304).

8.4.2 Multi-storey Shear Structure

A six-storey shear structure can be visualized in Fig. 8.16. In this example, the mass and stiffness parameters are chosen as $m_1 = 90\,\text{kg}$, $m_2 = 75\,\text{kg}$, $m_3 = 85\,\text{kg}$, $m_4 = 70\,\text{kg}$, $m_5 = 90\,\text{kg}$, $m_6 = 80\,\text{kg}$ and $k_1 = 820$ N/m, $k_2 = 1100\,\text{N/m}$, $k_3 = 1210\,\text{N/m}$, $k_4 = 1200\,\text{N/m}$, $k_5 = 1000\,\text{N/m}$, $k_6 = 800\,\text{N/m}$, respectively.

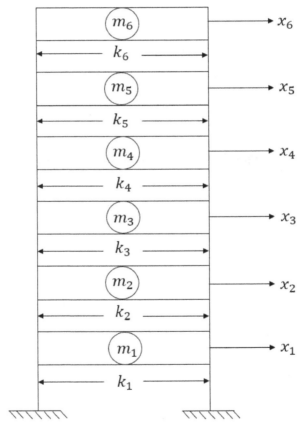

Fig. 8.16. Six-storey shear structure.

The mass and stiffness matrices for this example can be found as

$$M = \begin{bmatrix} 90 & 0 & 0 & 0 & 0 & 0 \\ 0 & 75 & 0 & 0 & 0 & 0 \\ 0 & 0 & 85 & 0 & 0 & 0 \\ 0 & 0 & 0 & 70 & 0 & 0 \\ 0 & 0 & 0 & 0 & 90 & 0 \\ 0 & 0 & 0 & 0 & 0 & 80 \end{bmatrix} \text{ and}$$

$$K = \begin{bmatrix} 1920 & -1100 & 0 & 0 & 0 & 0 \\ -1100 & 2310 & -1210 & 0 & 0 & 0 \\ 0 & -1210 & 2410 & -1200 & 0 & 0 \\ 0 & 0 & -1200 & 2200 & -1000 & 0 \\ 0 & 0 & 0 & -1000 & 1800 & -800 \\ 0 & 0 & 0 & 0 & -800 & 800 \end{bmatrix}$$

From Eq. (8.8), the coefficient matrix is calculated as

$$A = M^{-1}K = \begin{bmatrix} 21.3333 & -12.2222 & 0 & 0 & 0 & 0 \\ -14.6667 & 30.8000 & -16.1333 & 0 & 0 & 0 \\ 0 & -14.2353 & 28.3529 & -14.1176 & 0 & 0 \\ 0 & 0 & -17.1429 & 31.4286 & -14.2857 & 0 \\ 0 & 0 & 0 & -11.1111 & 20.0000 & -8.8889 \\ 0 & 0 & 0 & 0 & -10.0000 & 10.0000 \end{bmatrix}$$

In this case, the characteristic polynomial is given by

$$\lambda^6 - 141.9148\lambda^5 + 7323.6513\lambda^4 - 168771.8842\lambda^3 + 1708912.4678\lambda^2 \\ - 6158926.9350\lambda + 3623357.5686 = 0 \qquad (8.10)$$

ANN-based technique is applied to handle Eq. (8.10). Again, initial weights and learning parameters along with the computed eigenvalues have been given in Table 8.4. Convergence plots of the eigenvalues have been shown in Figs. 8.17–8.22.

Table 8.4. Eigenvalues using ANN procedure.

	Initial Weight	Learning Parameter(η)	Eigenvalue
λ_1	0.01	10^{-11}	0.7235
λ_2	4.1	10^{-10}	5.8920
λ_3	12	10^{-10}	15.3973
λ_4	23	10^{-10}	25.1417
λ_5	36	10^{-11}	40.3685
λ_6	51	10^{-12}	54.3918

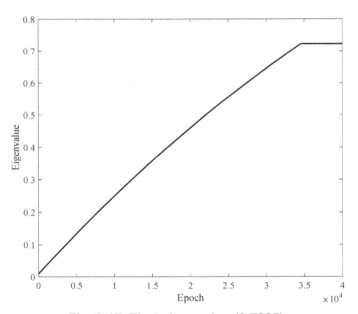

Fig. 8.17. First eigenvalue (0.7235).

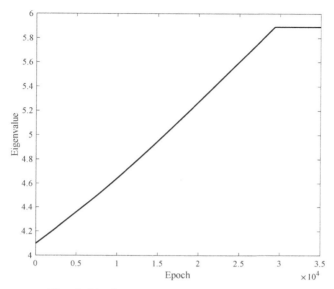

Fig. 8.18. Second eigenvalue (5.8920).

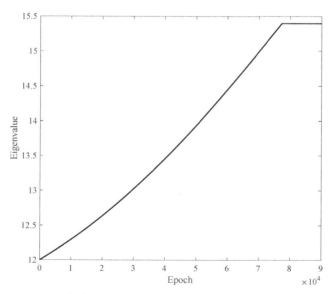

Fig. 8.19. Third eigenvalue (15.3973).

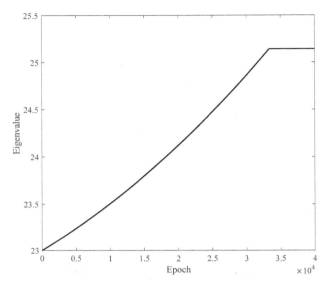

Fig. 8.20. Fourth eigenvalue (25.1417).

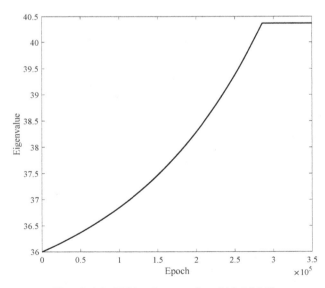

Fig. 8.21. Fifth eigenvalue (40.3685).

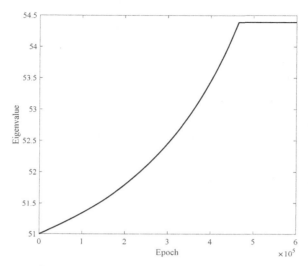

Fig. 8.22. Sixth eigenvalue (54.3918).

In this section, two application problems of structural dynamics viz. Four-degrees-of-freedom spring mass system and six-storey shear structure have been investigated using the ANN method. Frequency parameters (eigenvalues) have been computed in both the problems. The eigenvalues found in these problems may be verified by putting these in the respective characteristic polynomials.

8.5 Conclusion

In this chapter, a novel approach based on the concept of ANN has been addressed for solving eigenvalue problems. Further, the detailed ANN architecture to handle the eigenvalue problems has also been presented. Two mathematical examples along with two application problems of structural dynamics have been investigated.

References

[1] Y. Saad, (1992). *Numerical methods for large eigenvalue problems*. Manchester University Press.

[2] G. Strang, (1993). *Introduction to linear algebra* (Vol. 3). Wellesley, MA: Wellesley-Cambridge Press.

[3] J. J. Dongarra, I. S. Duff, D. C. Sorensen, and H. A. Van der Vorst, (1998). *Numerical linear algebra for high-performance computers* (Vol. 7). Siam.

[4] R. B. Bhat and S. Chakraverty, (2004). Numerical analysis in engineering. Alpha Science Int'l Ltd.

[5] D. S. Watkins, (2007). The matrix eigenvalue problem: GR and Krylov subspace methods (Vol. 101). Siam.

[6] S. H. Gould, (2012). Variational methods for eigenvalue problems: An introduction to the methods of Rayleigh, Ritz, Weinstein, and Aronszajn. Courier Corporation.

[7] G. L. Sleijpen and H. A. Van der Vorst, (2000). A Jacobi--Davidson iteration method for linear eigenvalue problems. *SIAM Review*, *42*(2), 267–293.

[8] A. Cichocki and R. Unbehauen, (1992). Neural networks for computing eigenvalues and eigenvectors. *Biological Cybernetics*, *68*(2), 155–164.

[9] N. Samardzija and R. L. Waterland, (1991). A neural network for computing eigenvectors and eigenvalues. *Biological Cybernetics*, *65*(4), 211–214.

[10] Z. Yi, Y. Fu, and H. J. Tang, (2004). Neural networks based approach for computing eigenvectors and eigenvalues of symmetric matrix. *Computers & Mathematics with Applications*, *47*(8–9), 1155–1164.

[11] F. Feng, Q. Zhang, and H. Liu, (2005). A recurrent neural network for extreme eigenvalue problem. In *International Conference on Intelligent Computing* (pp. 787–796). Springer, Berlin, Heidelberg.

[12] T. Q. Bui, M. N. Nguyen, and C. Zhang, (2011). A moving Kriging interpolation-based element-free Galerkin method for structural dynamic analysis. *Computer Methods in Applied Mechanics and Engineering*, *200*(13–16), 1354–1366.

[13] J. Kuan-Jung, and E. L. Wilson, (1988). An adaptive finite element technique for structural dynamic analysis. *Computers & structures*, *30*(6), 1319–1339.

[14] C. P. Providakis and D. E. Beskos, (1986). Dynamic analysis of beams by the boundary element method. *Computers & structures*, *22*(6), 957–964.

[15] R. K. Moghadas, and S. Gholizadeh, (2008). A new wavelet back propagation neural networks for structural dynamic analysis. *Engineering Letters*, *16*(1).

[16] S. K. Jeswal and S. Chakraverty, (2020). Eigenvalue problems of structural dynamics using ANN. In *Recent Trends in Wave Mechanics and Vibrations* (pp. 343–360). Springer, Singapore.

[17] J. P. Wolf, (1994). *Foundation vibration analysis using simple physical models*. Pearson Education.

[18] C. Beards, (1996). *Structural vibration: Analysis and damping*. Elsevier.

[19] S. Chakraverty, (2008). *Vibration of plates*. CRC press.

[20] S. Chakraverty and L. Behera, (2016). Static and dynamic problems of nanobeams and nanoplates. World Scientific.

[21] N. O. Myklestad, (2018). *Fundamentals of vibration analysis*. Courier Dover Publications.

9

Nonlinear Eigenvalue Problems with Application in Structural Dynamics

ANN technique for solving Nonlinear Eigenvalue Problems (NEPs) has been addressed in this chapter. Firstly, a numerical example of NEP has been solved using the ANN method. It is worth mentioning that dynamic analysis of structures with damping may lead to NEPs. As such, the application problem of spring mass system with damping has been investigated using the above said ANN procedure. Convergence plots for the computed eigenvalues have also been shown.

9.1 Introduction

Nonlinear eigenvalue problems have seen a great interest for research over the years. They have a wide range of applications in engineering and science viz. dynamic analysis of structures, photonic crystals, mechanics and gas dynamics equations, etc. Although, various methods have been developed and studied for linear eigenvalue problems, the NEPs have not been studied much. Accordingly, the ANN method for solving NEPs has been discussed here.

Solution of NEPs has been proposed by various researchers. In this regard, a novel Jacobi–Davidson-type projection method for NEPs has been proposed by Betcke and Voss [1]. An iterative method for computing the smallest eigenvalue of symmetric NEPs has been introduced by Solov'ëv [2]. Liao *et al*. [3] presented a nonlinear Rayleigh–Ritz iterative method for solving large-scale NEPs. A successive quadratic approximations method has been developed by Qian *et al*. [4]. Jia *et al*. [5] addressed a full multigrid method. A polynomial method based on the concept of Chebyshev interpolation has been studied by Effenberger and Kressner [6]. Various other methods have also been proposed such as Arnoldi method [7], block Newton method [8], improved Newton method [9], etc. to handle NEPs.

As we know, dynamic analysis of structures with damping may reduce to NEPs. In this context, Daya and Potier-Ferry [10] presented a method based on homotopy and asymptotic numerical techniques to find the natural frequencies of viscoelastic structures. An ANN method for solving NEPs of structural dynamics has been proposed by Jeswal and Chakraverty [11].

9.2 Nonlinear Eigenvalue Problem (NEP)

NEP may be defined as

$$A(\lambda)x = 0 \tag{9.1}$$

where λ is the eigenvalue and x is the eigenvector corresponding to the eigenvalue λ. Here, $A(\lambda)$ is the matrix-valued nonlinear function of λ. The general form of NEP (9.1) of degree n is written as follows:

$$A(\lambda)x = \sum_{i=0}^{n} \lambda^i A_i x = (A_0 + A_1\lambda + \cdots + A_{n-1}\lambda^{n-1} + A_n\lambda^n)x = 0 \tag{9.2}$$

where the coefficients A_i for $i = 0, 1, \cdots, n$ are square matrices.

Depending upon the degree of λ, there exist different forms of NEPs such as

- Quadratic eigenvalue problem (QEP):

$$A(\lambda)x = (A_0 + A_1\lambda + A_2\lambda^2)x = 0$$

- Cubic eigenvalue problem:

$$A(\lambda)x = (A_0 + A_1\lambda + A_2\lambda^2 + A_3\lambda^3)x = 0, \text{ etc.}$$

The QEP may be converted to generalized eigenvalue problem (GEP) as [12]

$$\begin{bmatrix} 0 & I \\ -A_0 & -A_1 \end{bmatrix} x = \lambda \begin{bmatrix} I & 0 \\ 0 & A_2 \end{bmatrix} x \tag{9.3}$$

The above GEP reduces to standard eigenvalue problem (SEP) by multiplying the inverse of the right-hand side matrix on both sides of Eq. (9.3).

Characteristic polynomial for Eq. (9.3) can be written as

$$a_1\lambda + a_2\lambda^2 + \cdots + a_n\lambda^n = c \qquad (9.4)$$

where $a_1, a_2, \cdots, a_n$ are the different coefficients and c is the constant term.

9.3 Numerical Example

In this section, a numerical example of NEP has been solved using the ANN procedure (Section 3.2.1, Chapter 3). Convergence plots for the computed eigenvalues have also been demonstrated.

Example 9.1: Let us consider an NEP [13]

$$N(X) = \begin{bmatrix} 1 & 0 \\ 0 & 1 \end{bmatrix} X^2 + \begin{bmatrix} -1 & -6 \\ 2 & -9 \end{bmatrix} X + \begin{bmatrix} 0 & 12 \\ -2 & 14 \end{bmatrix} \qquad (9.5)$$

Equation (9.5) can be linearized as

$$\begin{bmatrix} 0 & 0 & 1 & 0 \\ 0 & 0 & 0 & 1 \\ 0 & -12 & 1 & 6 \\ 2 & -14 & -2 & 9 \end{bmatrix} X = \lambda X \qquad (9.6)$$

The characteristic polynomial of Eq. (9.6) may be obtained as

$$\lambda^4 - 10\lambda^3 + 35\lambda^2 - 50\lambda + 24 = 0 \qquad (9.7)$$

Equation (9.7) can be solved using the ANN procedure. The parameters used in the ANN procedure viz. initial weights and learning parameters along with the computed eigenvalues have been included in Table 9.1. Convergence plots of the different eigenvalues have been illustrated in Fig. 9.1.

Table 9.1. Eigenvalues of NEP (9.5) using ANN procedure.

	Initial Weight	Learning Parameter(η)	Eigenvalues (λ)
λ_1	0.1	0.01	1.0000
λ_2	1.4	0.1	2.0000
λ_3	2.55	0.1	3.0000
λ_4	3.7	0.01	4.0000

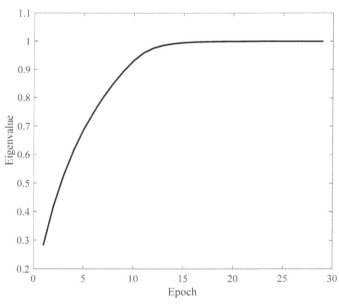

(a) First eigenvalue (1.0000)

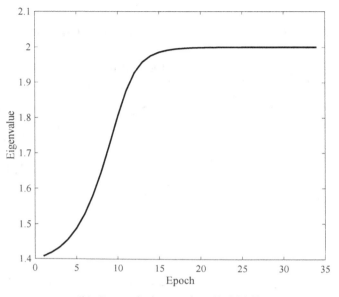

(b) Second eigenvalue (2.0000)

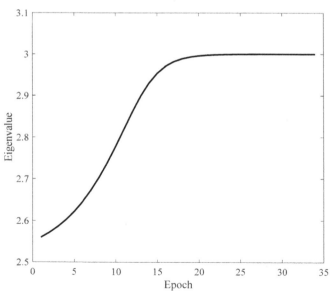

(c) Third eigenvalue (3.0000)

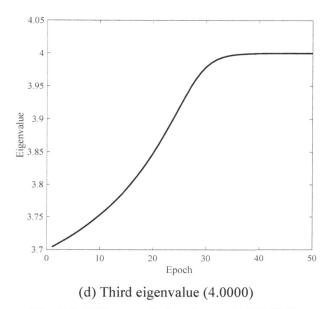

(d) Third eigenvalue (4.0000)

Fig. 9.1. Different eigenvalues of NEP (9.5).

It may be seen from the above example that the ANN method is helpful in solving NEPs. The eigenvalues obtained using the ANN method are the same as given in [13]. Moreover, the computed eigenvalues may also be verified by putting these in Eq. (9.7).

As mentioned earlier, dynamic analysis of structures with damping may lead to NEPs. In this context, two example problems of spring mass system have been examined in the following section. The ANN procedure (Section 3.2.1, Chapter 3) is applied to find the eigenvalues.

9.4 Application Problem

The general equation for dynamic analysis of structure (free vibration) is [14–17]

$$[M][\ddot{x}] + [C][\dot{x}] + [K][x] = 0 \tag{9.8}$$

where $[M]$, $[C]$ and $[K]$ are the mass, damping and stiffness matrices, respectively, which can be written as

$$M = \begin{bmatrix} m_1 & 0 & 0 & \cdots & 0 \\ 0 & m_2 & 0 & \cdots & 0 \\ \cdots & \cdots & \ddots & \cdots & \cdots \\ 0 & \cdots & 0 & m_{n-1} & 0 \\ 0 & \cdots & \cdots & 0 & m_n \end{bmatrix}, \quad C = \begin{bmatrix} c_1 + c_2 & -c_2 & 0 & \cdots & 0 \\ -c_2 & c_2 + c_3 & -c_3 & \cdots & 0 \\ \cdots & \cdots & \ddots & \cdots & \cdots \\ 0 & \cdots & -c_{n-1} & c_{n-1} + c_n & -c_n \\ 0 & \cdots & \cdots & -c_n & c_n \end{bmatrix}$$

$$K = \begin{bmatrix} k_1 + k_2 & -k_2 & 0 & \cdots & 0 \\ -k_2 & k_2 + k_3 & -k_3 & \cdots & 0 \\ \cdots & \cdots & \ddots & \cdots & \cdots \\ 0 & \cdots & -k_{n-1} & k_{n-1} + k_n & -k_n \\ 0 & \cdots & \cdots & -k_n & k_n \end{bmatrix}.$$

Equation (9.8) can be transformed into NEP as

$$(M\lambda^2 + C\lambda + K)x = 0 \tag{9.9}$$

Now, Eq. (9.9) may be converted to a GEP as [12]

$$\begin{bmatrix} [0] & [I] \\ -[K] & -[C] \end{bmatrix} x = \lambda \begin{bmatrix} [I] & [0] \\ [0] & [M] \end{bmatrix} x \tag{9.10}$$

Now, Eq. (9.10) can be solved using the ANN procedure.

An n-dimensional damped spring mass system [12] has been considered as shown in Fig. 9.2. In this case, the different matrices involved in Eq. (9.9) are real symmetric. The ith mass M_i is connected to $(i+1)$th mass by a damper and spring with constants C_i and K_i respectively. Further, the ith mass is connected to ground by a damper and spring with constants τ_i and k_i, respectively. For this spring mass system, the dynamic analysis gives rise to a second-order differential equation. In this case, the mass, damping and stiffness matrices can be defined as [12]

$$M = diag(M_1, M_2, \cdots, M_n)$$

$$C = B\,diag(C_1, C_2, \cdots, C_{n-1}, 0) + diag(\tau_1, \tau_2, \cdots, \tau_n)$$

$$K = B\,diag(K_1, K_2, \cdots, K_{n-1}, 0) + diag(k_1, k_2, \cdots, k_n)$$

respectively, where $B = \delta_{ij} - \delta_{i,j+1}$ (δ_{ij} is the Kronecker delta).

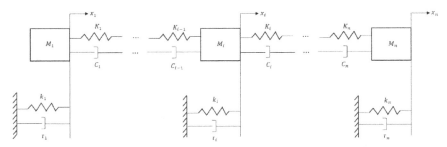

Fig. 9.2. *n*-dimensional spring mass system [12].

Next, two examples of the damped spring mass system have been investigated. In these examples, the spring and damper constants k, τ for first and last one are similar, that is $k_1 = k_n = 2k$ and $\tau_1 = \tau_n = 2\tau$, respectively [12]. For other cases, spring and damper constants will be k and τ. Lastly, the masses have been assumed as $M_i = 1$ [12].

Then, $M = I$, $C = \tau \, tridiag(-1,3,-1)$, $K = k \, tridiag(-1,3,-1)$.

Example 9.2: A damped spring mass system has been considered in this example with degree of freedom 3 (that is $n = 3$). Here, we have taken $\tau = 5$ and $k = 3$.

In this case, the mass, damping and stiffness matrices of Eq. (9.9) can be obtained as

$$M = \begin{bmatrix} 1 & 0 & 0 \\ 0 & 1 & 0 \\ 0 & 0 & 1 \end{bmatrix}, \; C = \begin{bmatrix} 15 & -5 & 0 \\ -5 & 15 & -5 \\ 0 & -5 & 15 \end{bmatrix} \text{ and } K = \begin{bmatrix} 9 & -3 & 0 \\ -3 & 9 & -3 \\ 0 & -3 & 9 \end{bmatrix}$$

Accordingly, the NEP can be written as

$$\left(\begin{bmatrix} 1 & 0 & 0 \\ 0 & 1 & 0 \\ 0 & 0 & 1 \end{bmatrix} \lambda^2 + \begin{bmatrix} 15 & -5 & 0 \\ -5 & 15 & -5 \\ 0 & -5 & 15 \end{bmatrix} \lambda + \begin{bmatrix} 9 & -3 & 0 \\ -3 & 9 & -3 \\ 0 & -3 & 9 \end{bmatrix} \right) x = 0 \quad (9.11)$$

Equation (9.11) can be written in SEP as

$$\begin{bmatrix} 0 & 0 & 0 & 1 & 0 & 0 \\ 0 & 0 & 0 & 0 & 1 & 0 \\ 0 & 0 & 0 & 0 & 0 & 1 \\ -9 & 3 & 0 & -15 & 5 & 0 \\ 3 & -9 & 3 & 5 & -15 & 5 \\ 0 & 3 & -9 & 0 & 5 & -15 \end{bmatrix} x = \lambda x \qquad (9.12)$$

Characteristic polynomial of Eq. (9.12) is given by

$$\lambda^6 + 45\lambda^5 + 652\lambda^4 + 3375\lambda^3 + 4950\lambda^2 + 2835\lambda + 567 = 0 \qquad (9.13)$$

Equation (9.13) has been solved using the ANN method to obtain the six eigenvalues. Table 9.2 includes the initial weights and learning parameters involved in the ANN method to find the eigenvalues. Obtained eigenvalues have also been incorporated in Table 9.2. The convergence plots of the different eigenvalues have been illustrated in Fig. 9.3.

Table 9.2. Eigenvalues of NEP (9.11) using ANN procedure.

	Initial Weight	Learning Parameter (η)	Eigenvalues (λ)
λ_1	-25	10^{-10}	-21.4538
λ_2	-13.2	10^{-9}	-14.3739
λ_3	-9	10^{-9}	-7.2750
λ_4	-1	10^{-3}	-0.6539
λ_5	-0.64	10^{-1}	-0.6261
λ_6	-0.4	10^{-3}	-0.6173

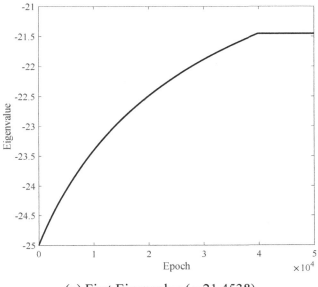

(a) First Eigenvalue (-21.4538)

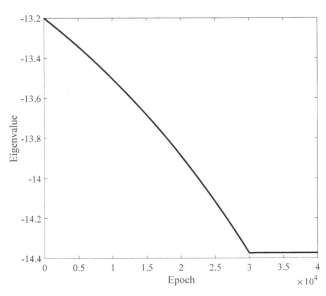

(b) Second Eigenvalue (-14.3739)

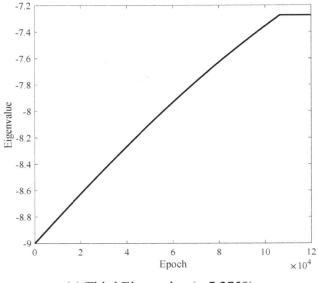

(c) Third Eigenvalue (-7.2750)

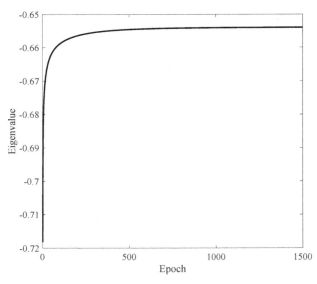

(d) Fourth Eigenvalue (-0.6539)

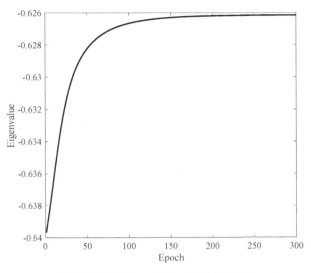

(e) Fifth Eigenvalue (-0.6261)

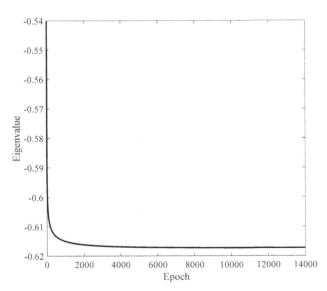

(f) Sixth Eigenvalue (-0.6173)

Fig. 9.3. Different eigenvalues of NEP (9.11).

Example 9.3: Let us consider a damped spring mass system having degree of freedom as three. Here we have assumed $\tau = 4$ and $k = 5$.

As such, the mass, damping and stiffness matrices of Eq. (9.9) can be found as

$$M = \begin{bmatrix} 1 & 0 & 0 \\ 0 & 1 & 0 \\ 0 & 0 & 1 \end{bmatrix}, \ C = \begin{bmatrix} 12 & -4 & 0 \\ -4 & 12 & -4 \\ 0 & -4 & 12 \end{bmatrix} \text{ and } K = \begin{bmatrix} 15 & -5 & 0 \\ -5 & 15 & -5 \\ 0 & -5 & 15 \end{bmatrix}$$

The NEP in this case is written as

$$\left(\begin{bmatrix} 1 & 0 & 0 \\ 0 & 1 & 0 \\ 0 & 0 & 1 \end{bmatrix} \lambda^2 + \begin{bmatrix} 12 & -4 & 0 \\ -4 & 12 & -4 \\ 0 & -4 & 12 \end{bmatrix} \lambda + \begin{bmatrix} 15 & -5 & 0 \\ -5 & 15 & -5 \\ 0 & -5 & 15 \end{bmatrix} \right) x = 0 \qquad (9.14)$$

Accordingly, SEP for Eq. (9.14) can be obtained as

$$\begin{bmatrix} 0 & 0 & 0 & 1 & 0 & 0 \\ 0 & 0 & 0 & 0 & 1 & 0 \\ 0 & 0 & 0 & 0 & 0 & 1 \\ -15 & 5 & 0 & -12 & 4 & 0 \\ 5 & -15 & 5 & 4 & -12 & 4 \\ 0 & -5 & 15 & 0 & 4 & -12 \end{bmatrix} x = \lambda x \qquad (9.15)$$

Characteristic polynomial of Eq. (9.15) can be found as

$$\lambda^6 + 36\lambda^5 + 445\lambda^4 + 2344\lambda^3 + 5665\lambda^2 + 6300\lambda + 2625 = 0 \qquad (9.16)$$

The ANN procedure is applied to solve Eq. (9.16). The initial weights, learning parameters used in the ANN method along with the computed eigenvalues have been included in Table 9.3. Further, convergence plots of the six eigenvalues have been depicted in Fig. 9.4.

Table 9.3. Eigenvalues of NEP (9.14) using ANN procedure.

	Initial Weight	Learning Parameter(η)	Eigenvalues (λ)
λ_1	-19	10^{-10}	-16.3031
λ_2	-12	10^{-9}	-10.5826
λ_3	-6	10^{-7}	$-.6310$
λ_4	-3.7	10^{-3}	-1.7121
λ_5	-1.6	10^{-2}	-1.4174
λ_6	-1	10^{-3}	-1.3538

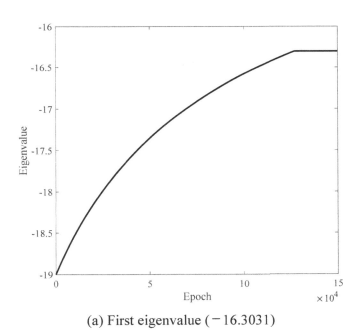

(a) First eigenvalue (-16.3031)

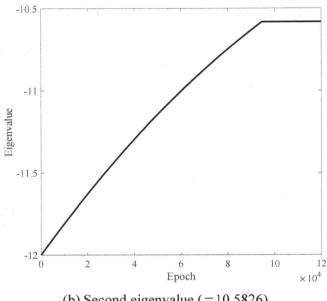

(b) Second eigenvalue (-10.5826)

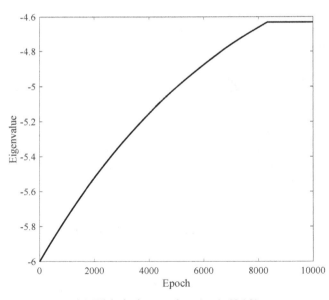

(c) Third eigenvalue (-4.6310)

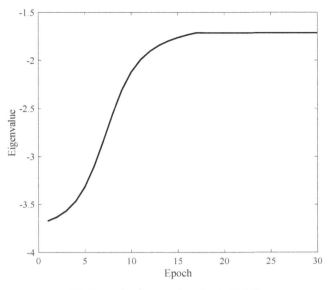

(d) Fourth eigenvalue (-1.7121)

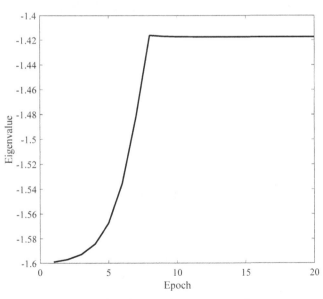

(e) Fifth eigenvalue (-1.4174)

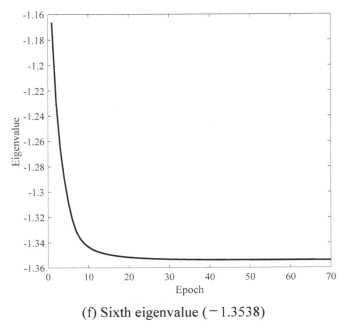

(f) Sixth eigenvalue (-1.3538)

Fig. 9.4. Different eigenvalues of NEP (9.14).

In this section, two examples of spring mass system have been investigated using the ANN method. Six eigenvalues have been computed in both the example problems. The eigenvalues obtained in these problems may be verified by putting these in the respective characteristic polynomials.

9.5 Conclusion

Nonlinear eigenvalue problems (NEPs) have been studied in this chapter. An ANN-based approach has been addressed here to handle the NEPs. The NEPs have been converted to SEPs and solved using the ANN procedure. A numerical example of NEP along with two example problems of the damped spring mass system has been investigated. Finally, convergence plots for different eigenvalues for the numerical example as well as application problems have also been depicted.

References

[1] T. Betcke and H. Voss, (2004). A Jacobi–Davidson-type projection method for nonlinear eigenvalue problems. *Future Generation Computer Systems*, *20*(3), 363–372.

[2] S. I. Solov'ëv (2006). Preconditioned iterative methods for a class of nonlinear eigenvalue problems. *Linear algebra and its applications*, *415*(1), 210–229.

[3] B. S. Liao, Z. Bai, L. Q. Lee, and K. Ko, (2010). Nonlinear Rayleigh-Ritz iterative method for solving large scale nonlinear eigenvalue problems. *Taiwanese Journal of Mathematics*, *14*(3A), 869–883.

[4] X. Qian, L. Wang, and Y. Song, (2015). A successive quadratic approximations method for nonlinear eigenvalue problems. *Journal of Computational and Applied Mathematics*, 290, 268–277.

[5] S. Jia, H. Xie, M. Xie, and F. Xu, (2016). A full multigrid method for nonlinear eigenvalue problems. *Science China Mathematics*, *59*(10), 2037–2048.

[6] C. Effenberger and D. Kressner, (2012). Chebyshev interpolation for nonlinear eigenvalue problems. *BIT Numerical Mathematics*, *52*(4), 933–951.

[7] H. Voss, (2004). An Arnoldi method for nonlinear eigenvalue problems. *BIT Numerical Mathematics*, *44*(2), 387–401.

[8] D. Kressner, (2009). A block Newton method for nonlinear eigenvalue problems. *Numerische Mathematik*, *114*(2), 355–372.

[9] S. A. Fazeli and F. Rabiei, (2016). Solving nonlinear eigenvalue problems using an improved newton method. *International Journal of Advanced Computer Science and Applications*, *7*(9), 438–441.

[10] E. M. Daya and M. Potier-Ferry, (2001). A numerical method for nonlinear eigenvalue problems application to vibrations of viscoelastic structures. *Computers & Structures*, *79*(5), 533–541.

[11] S. K. Jeswal and S. Chakraverty, (2019). Neural network approach for solving nonlinear eigenvalue problems of structural dynamics. *Neural Computing and Applications*, 1–9.

[12] F. Tisseur and K. Meerbergen, (2001). The quadratic eigenvalue problem. *SIAM Review*, *43*(2), 235–286.

[13] J. E. Dennis, Jr, J. F. Traub, and R. P. Weber, (1976). The algebraic theory of matrix polynomials. *SIAM Journal on Numerical Analysis*, *13*(6), 831–845.

[14] L. Meirovitch, (1975). *Elements of vibration analysis*. McGraw-Hill Science, Engineering & Mathematics.

[15] M. Petyt, (2010). *Introduction to finite element vibration analysis*. Cambridge university press.

[16] S. Chakraverty, (2008). *Vibration of plates*. CRC press. Boca Raton, FL.

[17] S. Chakraverty and K. K. Pradhan, (2018). *Computational structural mechanics: static and dynamic behaviors*. Academic Press. London.

10

Definite Integrals in the Fluid Force on a Vertical Surface

This chapter addresses an ANN-based technique for solving definite integrals. In this regard, single-layer Chebyshev Neural Network (ChNN) architecture has been considered where Chebyshev polynomials are used. Chebyshev polynomials are a sequence of orthogonal polynomials, which can be generated by a recursive formula. The main advantage of the ChNN method is the elimination of hidden layers by expanding the input patterns by Chebyshev polynomials that reduce the number of computations. In order to validate the proposed method, few numerical examples along with an application problem of fluid force on a vertical surface have been investigated.

10.1 Introduction

Definite integrals have several applications in various fields of engineering and science. Sometimes it is difficult to solve definite integrals because of the complicacy of the integral functions or it may require a lot of calculations to solve them. As such, the ChNN model may be helpful in solving definite integrals. Few applications of definite integrals can be used to estimate arc length of a curve, finding the area of a surface of revolution, the area between two curves, volumes of solids of revolution, etc.

Recently, various functional link neural network (FLNN)-based techniques have been developed to solve different problems. In this regard, an FLNN model where the removal of hidden layers has been done by expanding the input vector by Chebyshev polynomials has been proposed by Patra and Kot [1] for dynamic nonlinear system identification. Purwar *et al*. [2] used the Chebyshev Neural Network (ChNN) model for system identification of unknown dynamic nonlinear discrete time systems. A novel ChNN-based mechanism for modeling of complex DJ solar cell characteristics has been proposed by Patra [3]. A combination of ChNN and memristors have been proposed to perform function approximation by Wang *et al.* [4]. Zhou *et al.* [5] built a ChNN based on pattern recognition to predict Acute Hypotensive Episode (AHE) in ICU patients. Mall and Chakraverty [6] discussed ChNN-based technique to solve Lane–Emden type equations. Application of Legendre Neural Network for solving ordinary differential equations has been investigated by Mall and Chakraverty [7]. Further, ChNN model for solving elliptic partial differential equations has been examined by Mall and Chakraverty [8]. Mall and Chakraverty [9] presented a ChNN method for finding the numerical solution of nonlinear singular initial value problems of Emden–Fowler type. Yan *et al.* [10] discussed a spline basis function ANN algorithm for numerical integration. An ANN algorithm based on sine and cosine basis function to solve definite integrals has been proposed by Ying and Jun [11]. Recently, a book on solving ordinary differential equations based on different FLNN models has also been written by Chakraverty and Mall [12].

Although, few multi-layer ANN approaches [10, 11] to solve definite integrals have been proposed, they involve a lot of steps and may be computationally inefficient. As such, a single-layer ChNN model has been addressed here to solve definite integrals where the hidden layers have been removed by expanding the input patterns by Chebyshev polynomials.

10.2 Preliminaries

Integration is an important concept in the study of calculus. Moreover, integration is termed as the inverse operation of differentiation. Let f be a continuous real-valued function defined over an interval $[a,b]$ in the real line, then the definite integral can be defined as

$$\int_a^b f(x)dx = F(b) - F(a) \tag{10.1}$$

where $F'(x) = f(x)$ can be used to compute the definite integral.

Alternatively, definite integrals denote the area of the region in the

xy-plane that is bounded by the graph of f, the X-axis and the vertical lines $x = a$ and $x = b$.

In order to use ChNN, let us introduce the Chebyshev polynomials [13, 14], which are a set of orthogonal polynomials. The first few terms of Chebyshev polynomials of the first kind may be defined as

$t_0(x) = 1$

$t_1(x) = x$

$t_2(x) = 2x^2 - 1$

$t_3(x) = 4x^3 - 3x$

and so on.

Accordingly, the recursive formula for higher-order Chebyshev polynomials is written as [13]

$t_{n+1}(x) = 2xt_n(x) - t_{n-1}(x)$

where $t_n(x)$ is the nth order Chebyshev polynomial.

10.3 ChNN Methodology

An ANN architecture mainly consists of three layers viz. input, hidden and output. There may be more than one hidden layer in different instances. More number of hidden layers lead to more complications and computations. As such, a single-layer ANN model viz. Chebyshev Neural Network (ChNN) [2, 3] has been addressed for solving definite integrals. The single-layer ChNN architecture has been depicted in Fig. 10.1.

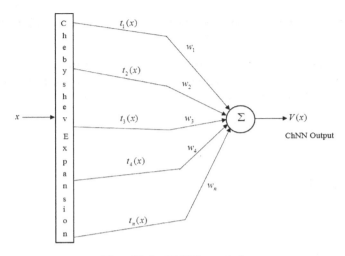

Fig. 10.1. ChNN model.

Here, the input vector is x, after expanding using Chebyshev polynomials, the input pattern can be transformed into a set element as $t_1(x), t_2(x), \cdots, t_n(x)$ corresponding to different weights $w_1, w_2, \cdots, w_n$, respectively.

The discussed model replaces $F(b)$ and $F(a)$ mentioned in Eq. (10.1) by $V(b)$ and $V(a)$, respectively. Moreover, $V(x)$ is the ChNN output. Hence, Eq. (10.1) can be rewritten as

$$\int_a^b f(x)dx = V(b) - V(a) \tag{10.2}$$

The ChNN output can be computed as

$$V(x) = w_1 t_1(x) + w_2 t_2(x) + \cdots + w_n t_n(x) \tag{10.3}$$

Here, $V(x)$ is constructed to approximate the function $F(x)$ up to the desired precision so the function $V(x)$ has been used later to calculate the values of the integral at a and b. Hence,

$$F(x) \approx V(x) \tag{10.4}$$

In some ideal situations, $F(x)$ equals to $V(x)$

$$F(x) - V(x) = 0 \tag{10.5}$$

Now, differentiating Eq. (10.5) with respect to x, we have

$$F'(x) - V'(x) = 0$$

Or it may equivalently be written as

$$f(x) - V'(x) = 0 \tag{10.6}$$

where $V'(x) = w_1 t_1'(x) + w_2 t_2'(x) + \cdots + w_n t_n'(x)$.

As such, Eq. (10.6) may be rewritten as

$$f(x) - (w_1 t_1'(x) + w_2 t_2'(x) + \cdots + w_n t_n'(x)) = 0 \tag{10.7}$$

Finally, the error term may be computed as

$$E = \frac{1}{2} \sum_{i=1}^{m} (f(x_i) - V'(x_i))^2 \tag{10.8}$$

where x_i are each training sample points; $m \in [a, b]$.

After calculating the error, the very next step involves weights updation which is given as follows:

Weight Updation:

Differentiating Eq. (10.8) with respect to different weights, we have

$$\frac{dE}{dw_k} = -\sum_{i=1}^{m} (f(x_i) - V'(x_i)) t_k'(x_i), \quad k = 1, 2, \cdots, n$$

Accordingly, the updating weights can be approximated as

$$w_k^{new} = w_k - \eta \frac{dE}{dw_k}, \quad k = 1, 2, \cdots, n$$

where η is the learning parameter.

10.4 Numerical Examples

This section solves two numerical examples of the definite integral using ChNN. The plots for the ChNN result of the examples have been demonstrated.

Example 10.1: Let us consider a definite integral

$$\int_0^{10} x^2 dx \tag{10.9}$$

which has the solution as 333.3333.

Equation (10.9) has now been solved using the ChNN method. Accordingly, ChNN model is trained with three Chebyshev polynomials viz. $t_1(x)$, $t_2(x)$ and $t_3(x)$. Three weights with respect to three Chebyshev polynomials are arbitrarily chosen as $w_1 = 0.7$, $w_2 = 0.8$ and $w_3 = 0.9$ with learning parameter 0.000001. In this case, ChNN result is obtained as 333.3333. Plot for the ChNN result has been shown in Fig. 10.2.

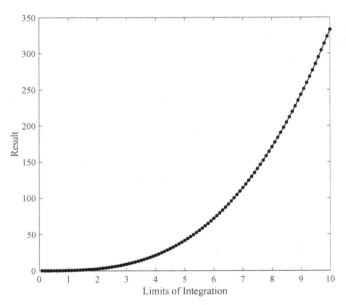

Fig. 10.2. ChNN result for problem (10.9).

Example 10.2: Another definite integral is considered as

$$\int_0^3 (x^2 + 1)dx$$

$$(10.10)$$

which has the solution as 12.

Four arbitrary weights viz. 0.1, 0.2, 0.3 and 0.4 with respect to the four Chebyshev polynomials are considered to solve Eq. (10.10) using the ChNN procedure. Further, the learning parameter is taken as 0.00001. As such, ChNN result is obtained as 12.0000 and corresponding plot is depicted in Fig. 10.3.

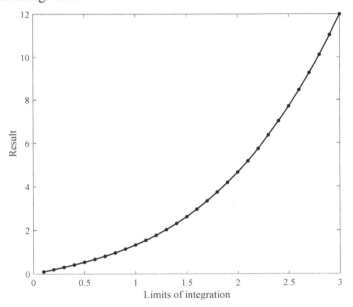

Fig. 10.3. ChNN result for problem (10.10).

Two examples of definite integrals have been solved using the ChNN procedure. The ChNN may be an alternative approach for solving definite integrals. Further, an application problem for definite integrals has been considered next.

10.5 Application Problem

Suppose a flat surface is submerged vertically in a fluid of weight density w and the submerged portion of the surface extends from $x = a$ to $x = b$ along the vertical X-axis, whose positive direction is taken as downward. If $L(x)$ is the width of the surface and $h(x)$ is the depth of point x, then the fluid force F is defined as [15]

$$F = \int_a^b wh(x)L(x)dx \qquad (10.11)$$

This formulation of the force on the side of a vertical surface works because liquids are virtually incompressible and the pressure on any part of an object (horizontal or vertical) at the same depth is the same.

An example of a vertical surface is the face of a dam. It can be visualized as a rectangle of a certain height and width, which is depicted in Fig. 10.4. Let the height and width of the dam be taken as 200 meters each, respectively. Here, we have to find the total fluid force exerted on the face if the top of the dam is level with the water surface.

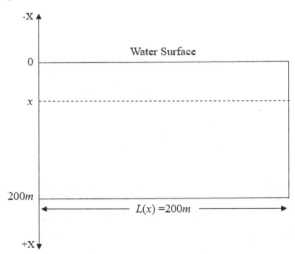

Fig. 10.4. Face of a dam.

Let x equal the depth of the water. At the depth x on the dam, the width of the dam is $L(x) = 200$ m and the depth is $h(x) = x$ m. The weighted density of water is

$$w_{water} = \rho g$$

$$= 1000 \times 9.8 = 9800 \ \text{N/m}^2$$

Using the fluid force formula above, we have

$$F = \int_a^b wh(x)L(x)dx$$

$$= \int_0^{200} (9800)(x)(200)dx$$

$$= 1960000 \int_0^{200} xdx \qquad (10.12)$$

The definite integral involved in Eq. (10.12) can be solved using the ChNN method. Here, the network is trained with two Chebyshev polynomials where weights along with learning parameter are chosen as 0.1, 0.2 and 0.000001, respectively. In this case, ChNN result is found to be 2×10^4 and corresponding plot has been illustrated in Fig. 10.5.

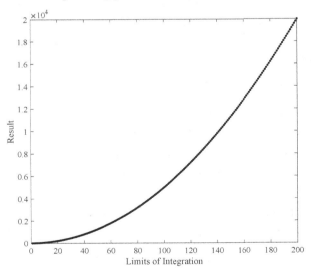

Fig. 10.5. ChNN result.

Finally, the total force on the vertical dam wall is obtained as 392×10^8 N.

10.6 Conclusion

An alternative ANN-based technique for solving definite integrals with the detailed procedure has been included. Accordingly, a single-layer Chebyshev Neural Network (ChNN) has been used. Hidden layer is removed by using the expansion of Chebyshev polynomials in the ChNN model. Two simple numerical example problems and an application problem have been solved to validate the method.

References

[1] J. C. Patra and A. C. Kot, (2002). Nonlinear dynamic system identification using Chebyshev functional link artificial neural networks. *IEEE Transactions on Systems, Man, and Cybernetics, Part B: Cybernetics, 32*(4), 505– 511.

[2] S. Purwar, I. N. Kar, and A. N. Jha, (2007). On-line system identification of complex systems using Chebyshev neural networks. *Applied Soft Computing, 7*(1), 364–372.

[3] J. C. Patra, (2011). Chebyshev neural network-based model for dual-junction solar cells. *IEEE Transactions on Energy Conversion, 26*(1), 132–139.

[4] L. Wang, M. Duan, and S. Duan, (2013). Memristive Chebyshev neural network and its applications in function approximation. *Mathematical Problems in Engineering,* 1–7. http://dx.doi.org/10.1155/2013/429402.

[5] Y. Zhou, Q. Zhu, and H. Huang, (2013). Prediction of Acute Hypotensive Episode in ICU using Chebyshev Neural Network. *JSW, 8*(8), 1923–1931.

[6] S. Mall and S. Chakraverty, (2014). Chebyshev neural network based model for solving Lane–Emden type equations. *Applied Mathematics and Computation, 247,* 100–114.

[7] S. Mall and S. Chakraverty, (2016). Application of Legendre Neural Network for solving ordinary differential equations. *Applied Soft Computing, 43*, 347–356.

[8] S. Mall and S. Chakraverty, (2017). Single layer Chebyshev neural network model for solving elliptic partial differential equations. *Neural Processing Letters, 45*(3), 825–840.

[9] S. Mall and S. Chakraverty (2015). Numerical solution of nonlinear singular initial value problems of Emden–Fowler type using Chebyshev Neural Network method. *Neurocomputing, 149*, 975–982.

[10] L. Yan, J. Di, and K. Wang, (2013). Spline basis neural network algorithm for numerical integration. *International Journal of Mathematical, Computational, Physical, Electrical and Computer Engineering, 7*(3), 458–461.

[11] L. Ying Xu and L. Jun Li, (2007). The new numerical integration algorithm based on neural network. *In Natural Computation, ICNC 2007. Third International Conference on IEEE, 1*, 325–328.

[12] S. Chakraverty and S. Mall, (2017). Artificial Neural Networks for Engineers and Scientists: Solving Ordinary Differential Equations. CRC Press.

[13] J. C. Mason and D. C. Handscomb (2002). Chebyshev polynomials. Chapman and Hall/CRC, Boca Raton, Florida.

[14] R. B. Bhat and S. Chakraverty, (2004). Numerical analysis in engineering. *Alpha Science Int'l Ltd*.

[15] R. Larson and B. H. Edwards, (2016). *Calculus of a single variable*. Nelson Education.

11

Inverse Problems in Structural Dynamics

This chapter discusses inverse problem of structural systems. In this regard, stiffness parameters are estimated using the ANN method for multi-degree of freedom systems with known masses. Two examples (discussed in Chapter 8) viz. spring mass system and multi-storey shear structure have been considered. Eigenvalues for these examples have already been calculated in Chapter 8. Eigenvectors corresponding to each eigenvalue have been computed using the ANN procedure (Section 6.2, Chapter 6). Accordingly, for known eigenvalues and eigenvectors, we have estimated the stiffness parameters where masses are known.

11.1 Introduction

Detection and identification of damage is an important aspect of structural systems. Structural damage detection may be considered an inverse problem. Here, an ANN-based approach has been discussed for solving the inverse problem.

Various techniques have been studied regarding the inverse problem of structures, but here few of them are discussed. In this regard, Gladwell [1] examined the inverse problem of lumped-mass system. Inverse eigenvalue problems associated with spring mass system have been investigated by Nylen and Uhlig [2, 3]. Tian and Li [4] discussed an inverse eigenvalue problem of star spring mass system. A genetic algorithm-based method has been proposed by Chou and Ghaboussi [5] for structural damage detection. Functional link neural network model has been developed to estimate the stiffness parameters of a multi-storey shear structure by Sahoo and Chakraverty [6]. Casciati [7] used differential evolution algorithms to investigate the inverse problem aiming at finding the stiffness of a structure. Ant colony optimization-based method has been addressed by Majumdar *et al.* [8] to determine the amount of damage in truss structures. Inverse problems of an axially vibrating rod are solved by Tian and Dai [9]. Inverse problems for 3-D multi-storey shear structures have been formulated and solved by Dolatshahi and Rofooei [10]. Chakraverty [11] presented a procedure to identify the mass and stiffness parameters from modal test data for multi-storey shear structures.

In order to understand the method of ANN for the inverse problems, we discuss the procedure in terms of numerical examples only.

11.2 Numerical Examples

Inverse problems of a four degree-of-freedom spring mass system and six-storey shear structure have been considered in this section. The eigenvalues of these problems have already been computed in Chapter 8. The eigenvectors corresponding to the computed eigenvalues have been obtained using the ANN method (Section 6.2, Chapter 6). As such, for known eigenvalues and eigenvectors, we have computed the coefficient matrix. Further, the stiffness matrix may be estimated using the known mass and coefficient matrices.

Example 11.1: In this example, inverse problem of four degree-of-freedom spring mass system (Section 8.4.1, Chapter 8) has been examined.

The eigenvectors for the spring mass system have been obtained using the ANN method. Four different linear systems have been derived for the four eigenvalues. The four linear systems have been solved using the ANN procedure to get the corresponding eigenvectors. For solving these systems, initial weights (guesses) have been chosen as [0.1; 0.1; 0.1; 0.1]. The learning parameters for solving these systems with computed eigenvectors have been included in Table 11.1.

Table 11.1. Computed eigenvectors using ANN procedure for Example 11.1.

λ_1	λ_2	λ_3	λ_4
1.0382	**3.8014**	**7.3444**	**12.8304**
$\begin{bmatrix} 0.0546 \\ 0.1027 \\ 0.1235 \\ 0.0923 \end{bmatrix}$	$\begin{bmatrix} 0.0198 \\ 0.0251 \\ 0.0012 \\ -0.0280 \end{bmatrix}$	$\begin{bmatrix} 0.0300 \\ 0.0144 \\ -0.0362 \\ 0.0199 \end{bmatrix}$	$\begin{bmatrix} 0.0290 \\ -0.0214 \\ 0.0078 \\ -0.0017 \end{bmatrix}$
Learning Parameter $\eta = 0.006$	**Learning Parameter** $\eta = 0.01$	**Learning Parameter** $\eta = 0.01$	**Learning Parameter** $\eta = 0.005$

Now, we have four 4×4 linear systems with unknown coefficient matrix for the computed eigenvalues and eigenvectors pairs. The systems may be written as

$$\begin{bmatrix} a_{11} & a_{12} & a_{13} & a_{14} \\ a_{21} & a_{22} & a_{23} & a_{24} \\ a_{31} & a_{32} & a_{33} & a_{34} \\ a_{41} & a_{42} & a_{43} & a_{44} \end{bmatrix} \begin{bmatrix} 0.0546 \\ 0.1027 \\ 0.1235 \\ 0.0923 \end{bmatrix} = \begin{bmatrix} 0.0567 \\ 0.1066 \\ 0.1282 \\ 0.0958 \end{bmatrix}$$

$$\begin{bmatrix} a_{11} & a_{12} & a_{13} & a_{14} \\ a_{21} & a_{22} & a_{23} & a_{24} \\ a_{31} & a_{32} & a_{33} & a_{34} \\ a_{41} & a_{42} & a_{43} & a_{44} \end{bmatrix} \begin{bmatrix} 0.0198 \\ 0.0251 \\ 0.0012 \\ -0.0280 \end{bmatrix} = \begin{bmatrix} 0.0753 \\ 0.0954 \\ 0.0046 \\ -0.1064 \end{bmatrix}$$

$$\begin{bmatrix} a_{11} & a_{12} & a_{13} & a_{14} \\ a_{21} & a_{22} & a_{23} & a_{24} \\ a_{31} & a_{32} & a_{33} & a_{34} \\ a_{41} & a_{42} & a_{43} & a_{44} \end{bmatrix} \begin{bmatrix} 0.0300 \\ 0.0144 \\ -0.0362 \\ 0.0199 \end{bmatrix} = \begin{bmatrix} 0.2203 \\ 0.1058 \\ -0.2659 \\ 0.1462 \end{bmatrix}$$

$$\begin{bmatrix} a_{11} & a_{12} & a_{13} & a_{14} \\ a_{21} & a_{22} & a_{23} & a_{24} \\ a_{31} & a_{32} & a_{33} & a_{34} \\ a_{41} & a_{42} & a_{43} & a_{44} \end{bmatrix} \begin{bmatrix} 0.0290 \\ -0.0214 \\ 0.0078 \\ -0.0017 \end{bmatrix} = \begin{bmatrix} 0.3721 \\ -0.2746 \\ 0.1001 \\ -0.0218 \end{bmatrix}$$

The above four systems combined to form a 16×16 linear system. The ANN procedure is applied then to solve the 16×16 system to find the different unknown coefficients. The initial weights and learning parameter have been chosen as [0.1; 0.1; 0.1; 0.1; 0.1; 0.1; 0.1; 0.1; 0.1; 0.1; 0.1; 0.1; 0.1; 0.1; 0.1] and 0.9, respectively. Accordingly, the coefficient matrix is obtained as

$$A = \begin{bmatrix} 9.5078 & -4.5026 & 0.0015 & -0.0021 \\ -3.5955 & 6.7933 & -3.1985 & 00029 \\ 0.0022 & -2.6659 & 5.0014 & -2.3381 \\ 0.0013 & -0.0026 & -1.9976 & 3.7129 \end{bmatrix}$$

From Eq. (8.8) (Chapter 8), it is known that $A = M^{-1}K$, hence the stiffness matrix may be computed as

$$K = MA = \begin{bmatrix} 380.3120 & -180.1040 & 0.0600 & -0.0840 \\ -179.7750 & 339.6650 & -159.9250 & 0.1450 \\ 0.1320 & -159.9540 & 300.0840 & -140.2860 \\ 0.0910 & -0.1820 & -139.8320 & 259.8820 \end{bmatrix}$$

The obtained stiffness matrix as above is almost similar to that of the spring mass system in Chapter 8.

Example 11.2: Inverse problem of a six-storey shear structure (Section 8.4.2, Chapter 8) has been investigated in this example.

The ANN method has been applied to find the eigenvectors for the six-storey shear structure. Six different linear systems have been obtained corresponding to the six eigenvalues. These systems have been solved using the ANN procedure to obtain the eigenvectors. The initial weights for solving the six systems have been chosen as [0.1; 0.1; 0.1; 0.1; 0.1; 0.1]. The learning parameters for solving the linear systems with computed eigenvectors have been incorporated in Table 11.2.

Table 11.2. Computed eigenvectors using ANN procedure for Example 11.2.

λ_1	λ_2	λ_3	λ_4	λ_5	λ_6
0.7235	**5.8920**	**15.3973**	**25.1417**	**40.3685**	**54.3918**
$\begin{bmatrix} 0.0385 \\ 0.0649 \\ 0.0860 \\ 0.1029 \\ 0.1179 \\ 0.1271 \end{bmatrix}$	$\begin{bmatrix} 0.0289 \\ 0.0365 \\ 0.0301 \\ 0.0111 \\ -0.0163 \\ -0.0398 \end{bmatrix}$	$\begin{bmatrix} 0.0169 \\ 0.0082 \\ -0.0075 \\ -0.0152 \\ -0.0080 \\ 0.0148 \end{bmatrix}$	$\begin{bmatrix} 0.0041 \\ -0.0013 \\ -0.0041 \\ 0.0003 \\ 0.0051 \\ -0.0034 \end{bmatrix}$	$\begin{bmatrix} 0.0050 \\ -0.0078 \\ 0.0001 \\ 0.0078 \\ -0.0050 \\ 0.0016 \end{bmatrix}$	$\begin{bmatrix} -0.0029 \\ 0.0078 \\ -0.0088 \\ 0.0084 \\ -0.0029 \\ 0.0006 \end{bmatrix}$
Learning Parameter $\eta = 0.0001$	Learning Parameter $\eta = 0.0001$	Learning Parameter $\eta = 0.001$	Learning Parameter $\eta = 0.001$	Learning Parameter $\eta = 0.001$	Learning Parameter $\eta = 0.0001$

Further, six 6×6 linear systems have been obtained from the six eigenvalues with their corresponding eigenvectors. These six systems may be written as

$$
\begin{bmatrix}
a_{11} & a_{12} & a_{13} & a_{14} & a_{15} & a_{16} \\
a_{21} & a_{22} & a_{23} & a_{24} & a_{25} & a_{26} \\
a_{31} & a_{32} & a_{33} & a_{34} & a_{35} & a_{36} \\
a_{41} & a_{42} & a_{43} & a_{44} & a_{45} & a_{46} \\
a_{51} & a_{52} & a_{53} & a_{54} & a_{55} & a_{56} \\
a_{61} & a_{62} & a_{63} & a_{64} & a_{65} & a_{66}
\end{bmatrix}
\begin{bmatrix}
0.0385 \\
0.0649 \\
0.0860 \\
0.1029 \\
0.1179 \\
0.1271
\end{bmatrix}
=
\begin{bmatrix}
0.0279 \\
0.0470 \\
0.0622 \\
0.0744 \\
0.0853 \\
0.0920
\end{bmatrix}
$$

$$
\begin{bmatrix}
a_{11} & a_{12} & a_{13} & a_{14} & a_{15} & a_{16} \\
a_{21} & a_{22} & a_{23} & a_{24} & a_{25} & a_{26} \\
a_{31} & a_{32} & a_{33} & a_{34} & a_{35} & a_{36} \\
a_{41} & a_{42} & a_{43} & a_{44} & a_{45} & a_{46} \\
a_{51} & a_{52} & a_{53} & a_{54} & a_{55} & a_{56} \\
a_{61} & a_{62} & a_{63} & a_{64} & a_{65} & a_{66}
\end{bmatrix}
\begin{bmatrix}
0.0289 \\
0.0365 \\
0.0301 \\
0.0111 \\
-0.0163 \\
-0.0398
\end{bmatrix}
=
\begin{bmatrix}
0.1703 \\
0.2151 \\
0.1773 \\
0.0654 \\
-0.0960 \\
-0.2345
\end{bmatrix}
$$

$$
\begin{bmatrix}
a_{11} & a_{12} & a_{13} & a_{14} & a_{15} & a_{16} \\
a_{21} & a_{22} & a_{23} & a_{24} & a_{25} & a_{26} \\
a_{31} & a_{32} & a_{33} & a_{34} & a_{35} & a_{36} \\
a_{41} & a_{42} & a_{43} & a_{44} & a_{45} & a_{46} \\
a_{51} & a_{52} & a_{53} & a_{54} & a_{55} & a_{56} \\
a_{61} & a_{62} & a_{63} & a_{64} & a_{65} & a_{66}
\end{bmatrix}
\begin{bmatrix}
0.0169 \\
0.0082 \\
-0.0075 \\
-0.0152 \\
-0.0080 \\
0.0148
\end{bmatrix}
=
\begin{bmatrix}
0.2602 \\
0.1263 \\
-0.1155 \\
-0.2340 \\
-0.1232 \\
0.2279
\end{bmatrix}
$$

$$
\begin{bmatrix}
a_{11} & a_{12} & a_{13} & a_{14} & a_{15} & a_{16} \\
a_{21} & a_{22} & a_{23} & a_{24} & a_{25} & a_{26} \\
a_{31} & a_{32} & a_{33} & a_{34} & a_{35} & a_{36} \\
a_{41} & a_{42} & a_{43} & a_{44} & a_{45} & a_{46} \\
a_{51} & a_{52} & a_{53} & a_{54} & a_{55} & a_{56} \\
a_{61} & a_{62} & a_{63} & a_{64} & a_{65} & a_{66}
\end{bmatrix}
\begin{bmatrix}
0.0041 \\
-0.0013 \\
-0.0041 \\
0.0003 \\
0.0051 \\
-0.0034
\end{bmatrix}
=
\begin{bmatrix}
0.1031 \\
-0.0327 \\
-0.1031 \\
0.0075 \\
0.1282 \\
-0.0855
\end{bmatrix}
$$

$$\begin{bmatrix} a_{11} & a_{12} & a_{13} & a_{14} & a_{15} & a_{16} \\ a_{21} & a_{22} & a_{23} & a_{24} & a_{25} & a_{26} \\ a_{31} & a_{32} & a_{33} & a_{34} & a_{35} & a_{36} \\ a_{41} & a_{42} & a_{43} & a_{44} & a_{45} & a_{46} \\ a_{51} & a_{52} & a_{53} & a_{54} & a_{55} & a_{56} \\ a_{61} & a_{62} & a_{63} & a_{64} & a_{65} & a_{66} \end{bmatrix} \begin{bmatrix} 0.0050 \\ -0.0078 \\ 0.0001 \\ 0.0078 \\ -0.0050 \\ 0.0016 \end{bmatrix} = \begin{bmatrix} 0.2018 \\ -0.3149 \\ 0.0040 \\ 0.3149 \\ -0.2018 \\ 0.0646 \end{bmatrix}$$

$$\begin{bmatrix} a_{11} & a_{12} & a_{13} & a_{14} & a_{15} & a_{16} \\ a_{21} & a_{22} & a_{23} & a_{24} & a_{25} & a_{26} \\ a_{31} & a_{32} & a_{33} & a_{34} & a_{35} & a_{36} \\ a_{41} & a_{42} & a_{43} & a_{44} & a_{45} & a_{46} \\ a_{51} & a_{52} & a_{53} & a_{54} & a_{55} & a_{56} \\ a_{61} & a_{62} & a_{63} & a_{64} & a_{65} & a_{66} \end{bmatrix} \begin{bmatrix} -0.0029 \\ 0.0078 \\ -0.0088 \\ 0.0084 \\ -0.0029 \\ 0.0006 \end{bmatrix} = \begin{bmatrix} -0.1577 \\ 0.4243 \\ -0.4786 \\ 0.4569 \\ -0.1577 \\ 0.0326 \end{bmatrix}$$

The above six systems have an unknown matrix with 36 unknown coefficients. As such, these six systems may be combined to get a 36×36 system to find the unknown coefficient matrix. Hence, the ANN method is implemented to solve the 36×36 system. In this case, initial weights are randomly selected as $[0.1; 0.1; \ldots; 0.1]$. Further, the learning parameter is chosen as 0.9. Accordingly, the coefficient matrix can be derived as

$$A = \begin{bmatrix} 21.3156 & -12.2282 & 0.0357 & -0.0247 & -0.0042 & 0.0065 \\ -14.5591 & 30.7605 & -16.1903 & -0.0057 & 0.0866 & -0.0478 \\ -0.0769 & -14.2158 & 28.4004 & -14.0833 & -0.0895 & 0.0398 \\ 0.0442 & 0.0127 & -17.2158 & 31.4388 & -14.2590 & -0.0116 \\ -0.0689 & 0.0088 & 0.0848 & -11.1774 & 20.0022 & -8.8750 \\ -0.0394 & -0.0091 & 0.1332 & -0.1357 & -9.9557 & 9.9953 \end{bmatrix}$$

Finally, the stiffness matrix can be found as

$$K = MA = \begin{bmatrix} 1918.4040 & -1100.5380 & 3.2130 & -2.2230 & -0.3780 & 0.5850 \\ -1091.9325 & 2307.0375 & -1214.2725 & -0.4275 & 6.4950 & -3.5850 \\ -6.5365 & -1208.3430 & 2414.0340 & -1197.0805 & -7.6075 & 3.3830 \\ 3.0940 & 0.8890 & -1205.1060 & 2200.7160 & -998.1300 & -0.8120 \\ -6.2010 & 0.7920 & 7.6320 & -1005.9660 & 1800.1980 & -798.7500 \\ -3.1520 & -0.7280 & 10.6560 & -10.8560 & -796.4560 & 799.6240 \end{bmatrix}$$

The obtained stiffness matrix is in good agreement with the matrix discussed earlier in case of the six-storey shear structure of Chapter 8.

11.3 Conclusion

The inverse problem of structural systems has been studied in this chapter. Here, the stiffness parameters are computed with known masses. In this regard, two examples of structural problems such as spring mass system and multi-storey shear structure have been investigated. The stiffness matrices obtained for the two examples are in good agreement with the matrices given in Chapter 8. It may be noted that in inverse problems there may be many other complexities for structural systems. But in this chapter, only an idea has been addressed for two simple example problems which may be extended to further challenging inverse problems.

References

[1] G. M. L. Gladwell, (1986). The inverse mode problem for lumped-mass systems. *The Quarterly Journal of Mechanics and Applied Mathematics*, *39*(2), 297–307.

[2] P. Nylen and F. Uhlig, (1997). Inverse eigenvalue problems associated with spring-mass systems. *Linear algebra and its applications*, *254*(1–3), 409–425.

[3] P. Nylen and F. Uhlig, (1997). Inverse eigenvalue problem: Existence of special spring-mass systems. *Inverse Problems*, *13*(4), 1071–1081.

[4] X. Tian and C. X. Li, (2012). An Inverse Eigenvalue Problem for Star Spring-Mass System. In *Applied Mechanics and Materials*, 166–169, 3348–3351.

[5] J. H. Chou and J. Ghaboussi, (2001). Genetic algorithm in structural damage detection. *Computers & structures, 79*(14), 1335–1353.

[6] D. M. Sahoo and S. Chakraverty, (2018). Functional link neural network approach to solve structural system identification problems. *Neural Computing and Applications, 30*(11), 3327–3338.

[7] S. Casciati, (2008). Stiffness identification and damage localization via differential evolution algorithms. *Structural Control and Health Monitoring: The Official Journal of the International Association for Structural Control and Monitoring and of the European Association for the Control of Structures, 15*(3), 436–449.

[8] A. Majumdar, D. K. Maiti, and D. Maity, (2012). Damage assessment of truss structures from changes in natural frequencies using ant colony optimization. *Applied Mathematics and Computation, 218*(19), 9759–9772.

[9] X. Tian and H. Dai, (2009). Inverse mode problems for the finite element model of a vibrating rod. *Applied Mathematics and Computation, 214*(2), 479–486.

[10] K. M. Dolatshahi and F. R. Rofooei, (2014). Inverse vibration problem for un-damped 3-dimensional multi-story shear building models. *Journal of Sound and Vibration, 333*(1), 99–113.

[11] S. Chakraverty, (2005). Identification of structural parameters of multistorey shear buildings from modal data. *Earthquake Engineering & Structural Dynamics, 34*(6), 543–554.

Index

C

D

Printed in the United States
by Baker & Taylor Publisher Services